303 Preschooler-Approved
Exercises and Active Games

303
Preschooler-Approved Exercises and Active Games

AGES 3-5

Kimberly Wechsler

Foreword by Tamilee Webb
Illustrated by Michael Sleva

A Hunter House SmartFun Book

I dedicate this book to the thousands of children who taught me how to bring together fitness and fun and to the children and families who will benefit from their teachings.

Hunter House Inc., Publishers
PO Box 2914
Alameda CA 94501-0914

Library of Congress Cataloging-in-Publication Data
Wechsler, Kimberly.
303 preschooler-approved exercises and active games : ages 3–5 /
Kimberly Wechsler. — First edition.
pages cm. — (SmartFun)
Contains index.
ISBN 978-0-89793-618-7 (pbk.) — ISBN 978-0-89793-623-1 (spiral)
1. Exercise for children. 2. Physical fitness for children. 3. Group games. I. Title.
II. Title: Three hundred and three preschooler-approved exercises and active games.
GV443.W39 2012
613.7′042—dc23
2012030032

Project Credits

Cover Design: Jinni Fontana	Publicity Coordinator: Martha Scarpati
Book Production: John McKercher	Rights Coordinator: Candace Groskreutz
Illustrator: Michael Sleva	Publisher's Assistant: Bronwyn Emery
Developmental and Copy Editor: Amy Bauman	Administrative Assistant: Kimberly Kim
Reviewer: Susan Lyn McCombs	Customer Service Manager: Christina Sverdrup
Proofreader: Lori Cavanaugh	Order Fulfillment: Washul Lakdhon
Managing Editor: Alexandra Mummery	Administrator: Theresa Nelson
Editorial Assistant: Tu-Anh Dang-Tran	Computer Support: Peter Eichelberger
Special Sales Manager: Judy Hardin	Publisher: Kiran S. Rana

Printed and bound by Bang Printing, Brainerd, Minnesota
Manufactured in the United States of America

9 8 7 6 5 4 3 2 1   First Edition   13 14 15 16 17

Contents

Introduction

The Exercises and Games

A list of the games indicating appropriate group sizes begins on the next page.

Please note that the illustrations in this book are all outline drawings. The fact that the pages are white does not imply that the people all have white skin. This book is for people of all races and ethnic identities.

List of Games

Kicking Skills

Bat-, Racquet-, and Golf-Swinging Skills

How to Teach Rhythm

Some Classic Dances and Single Steps

Most of the activities may be performed with groups of any size. A few are designed for pairs, small groups, or the whole group. These exceptions are individually marked with a group-size icon.

Foreword

Fitness has been an important part of my life since I was a little girl. With a father who played semi-pro baseball and three brothers, I wanted to keep up with the boys, and that meant playing sports, not playing with dolls! I believe this set the tone for how I would continue to live my life: striving to be fit and healthy! I'm grateful for parents who encouraged me to get involved with sports, which then led to an interest in fitness in general.

Children normally have lots of energy; like puppies, they want to run, jump, and have fun! They don't always know all that activity is good for their health, well-being, self-esteem, or coordination, but parents can set a good example and educate them along the way to give them a better chance of being healthy, fit adults! Kids love to learn and want to know how things work especially their own little bodies; don't pass up the chance to give them the book of health with Kimberly's *303 Preschooler-Approved Exercises and Active Games.*

I love motivating others to feel good in their bodies! I've been in the health and fitness industry for over 30 years, and I continue to lead group exercise classes in the San Diego area and produce fitness DVDs.

Tamilee Webb
Fitness instructor and star of *Buns of Steel, Abs of Steel*

Preface

What is worse than being an overweight adult? Being an overweight child. It's no secret that childhood obesity has become an epidemic in the United States within the last thirty years and is a contributing factor to serious health conditions such as heart disease, diabetes, hypertension, and other health issues regarding excess weight and obesity. Obesity is caused by a combination of excess calories, inactivity, and genetic predisposition. Not much can be done about genetic predisposition, but there is a great deal that families can do to promote a healthy home environment that encourages physical activity and healthy food choices that can reduce the risk of becoming overweight or obese.

As parents, teachers, coaches, and counselors, we have the power to help children live fit and healthy lifestyles. Not only can we help children shape their bodies, but we also can help them shape their attitudes and behaviors about living a healthy lifestyle. I have built a career on teaching fitness to children, teens, and adults. Exercise programs designed for families are not "one-size-fits-all" programs. Some movements that work well for one particular age group could prove disastrous for another. Each age group is uniquely different physiologically and intellectually, and each group is motivated by different factors. My mission as a family fitness specialist is to design exercise programs that provide and incorporate the latest research on health and fitness trends, take into consideration the best practices for each family member, and then offer a deep understanding and a big-picture perspective of keeping families fit.

In this book, I share my thoughts and the lessons I have learned about activating the children in your life. I am a parent, too, so I know firsthand the challenges American families face today in raising fit children. Through creative physical activities and opportunities, I will teach you how to turn your dynamic and hectic lifestyle into a healthy and active one. These books are not just for families with overweight children; they are for every family who understands how important it is to be active and live fit. In *303 Preschooler-Approved Exercises and Active Games*, *303 Kid-Approved Exercises and Active Games*, and *303 Tween-Approved Exercises and Active Games*, I am sharing more than 900 exercises. Each exercise is uniquely designed to fit the needs of a particular age group and each has been "kid approved" by the over 75,000 children and teens I have taught throughout my twenty years of teaching fitness. It is my hope that through this book you'll have all the information you need to lead the children in your life to active and healthy lives of their own.

— Kimberly Wechsler

For easy reading, we have alternated the use of male and female pronouns.
Of course, every "he" also includes "she," and vice versa.

Acknowledgments

I would like to thank my children, Andrew and Addison, for twenty years of being my "advisory board" on all fitness games. You can retire now; I promise I won't call you and ask for your opinions on fitness games—at least not tonight.

I would like to thank my friend and husband, Jonathan, for his loving support, his encouragement to follow my passion, his patience with my endless discussions about family fitness, and his many months of tireless proofreading.

I would like to thank First Lady Michelle Obama for commitment to the *Let's Move!* campaign: I have spoken about getting kids active for so long, but my voice alone wasn't strong enough to be heard. I prayed for a voice to be stronger than mine so that people everywhere would hear and understand the message that our children's health is worth fighting for. Thanks to you, people are listening.

My website is www.FitAmericanFamilies.com.

Important Note

The material in this book is intended to provide information about a safe, enjoyable program of physical games for children to play. Every effort has been made to provide accurate and dependable information. The contents of this book have been compiled through professional research and in consultation with professionals. However, professionals have differing opinions, and some of the information may become outdated; therefore, the publisher, authors, and editors, as well as the professionals quoted in the book, cannot be held responsible for any error, omission, or dated material. The authors and publisher assume no responsibility for any outcome of applying the information in this book. Follow the instructions closely. Note, too, that children's bodies differ, and no one should assume or be forced to assume any physical positions that cause pain or discomfort. If you have questions concerning an exercise or the application of the information described in this book, please consult a qualified medical professional.

Introduction

No doubt we've all heard the saying "It takes a village to raise a child." And most of us would agree that thought has more than a bit of truth to it. What that means—in part—is that raising a child can affect and is affected by everyone and everything around that child. Certainly if we think about that for a moment, we can see many ways in which that truth plays out for both the child AND the village.

In the same way, health—that of our children and even ourselves—affects those around us. And especially when it comes to our children, while it may or may not take a village to teach a child the way to a healthful life, the more people around our children who serve as good leaders and models—eating right, including activity in their everyday lives, and so on—the more easily children slip into those habits and behaviors themselves. No matter what your role is in that "village," there is a great deal that you can do.

Message to Parents, Teachers, Counselors

What if you could look into a crystal ball to see what the future holds for your child? Would you like to know? What if the crystal ball shows you that, in adulthood, your child is obese and faced with difficult challenges such as high blood pressure, high cholesterol, diabetes, and other weight-related issues? Is this the future you want for your child? Of course not; we all want only the best for our children. According to statistics from the U.S. Department of Health and Human Services, our children and teens are overweight or at risk for it, and studies blame the current obesity epidemic on our lifestyle choices, which include too many calories and over-the-top usage of television, the computer, and video games.

 Nothing is more important than the well-being of your child.

Nothing is more important than the well-being of your child. Let's take a look at how you can incorporate a more active lifestyle for your child at the preschool age.

The Scoop on Preschoolers

The preschool years, when children are between three and five years old, are filled with developmental milestones such as learning to tie a shoe, to follow simple instructions, and to catch or throw a ball. Preschool children develop physically, intellectually, emotionally, and socially. But different children grow and mature at different rates, especially between the ages of three and five years old. Girls sometimes grow faster than boys, so it is not beneficial to compare one child to another, but children in this age group do share common characteristics. For instance, children from three to five years old begin to develop lifestyle behaviors that can follow them all the way through adulthood. Therefore, it is vital to your child's health to instill healthy lifestyle habits, behaviors, and disciplines during these young years. The preschool years are also referred to as the years of development or the building-block years. The skills and behaviors a preschooler will learn during this phase of life lay the foundation upon which finer skills will build.

Because preschoolers come in all shapes and sizes, assessing a child's current state of health can be challenging. The best way to make this assessment, of course, is to consult a pediatrician. A child's pediatrician can address any and all questions about a child's current state of health and support any concerns about his well-being.

Understanding Children and BMI

Body mass index (BMI) is a number calculated from a child's weight and height; it is age and sex specific. BMI is a reliable indicator of body fat for most children and teens. It is an inexpensive and easy-to-perform method of screening for weight categories that may lead to health problems. After the BMI is calculated, the number is plotted on a chart with the age and sex of the child to obtain a percentile ranking. Percentiles are the most commonly used indicator to assess the size and growth patterns of individual children in the United States. The growth charts show the weight status categories used with children and teens such as underweight, healthy weight, overweight, and obese.

Addressing the At-Risk or Overweight Child

Without question, family behaviors can contribute to childhood obesity and inactive lifestyles. After all, kids aren't self-sufficient: They are not the ones who shop for food, drive the car to fast-food restaurants, or set the house rules about how much television they can watch. In addition, we, as families, cannot depend solely on others such as day-care providers, babysitters, personal trainers, coaches, and school systems to provide a preschooler with enough physical activity in a day or to ensure that a child is getting the nutritional food he needs in a day.

If a child is overweight, it is not just her problem; rather it is something the entire family must address, as the first line of defense is the home front. After consulting with a pediatrician, family members can choose appropriate games and activities from this book and, as a family, begin moving and playing toward a new lifestyle that is both active and fun.

Helping Children Become More Active

Preschoolers need opportunities for playful fitness—activities and movement that keep their bodies in motion—and for skill-building exercises such as chasing, jumping, crawling, climbing, and tumbling. Encourage a preschooler in an active healthy lifestyle and she will grow to love being physically active. And being physically active is an invaluable gift to give a child—one that keeps on giving even into adulthood. In striving to be fit, children will experience:

- increased energy expenditure
- strengthened muscles and bones
- improved cardiovascular endurance
- greater capacity to burn calories
- improved self-esteem
- decreased risk of serious illnesses later in life
- increased creative development
- practice with problem-solving skills
- improved motor-skill development
- opportunities for family involvement
- assistance in social development
- an understanding of the concept of sportsmanship
- practice with basic rule-following skills
- practice with receiving direction from someone outside of the family
- increased confidence
- developed cognitive thinking
- information on taking care of their bodies
- an awareness of their bodies
- better sleep habits
- a better appetite
- the ability to become more focused
- help in establishing friendships
- aid in developmental growth

What I Know about Preschoolers

As I have touched upon, each child is unique, and factors such as gender, age, and level of development need to be taken into consideration when developing an exercise plan. Be sure to select exercises and games that suit the needs and wants of your children.

What Preschoolers Need and Want in Physical Activity

- You. Preschoolers want and need adult attention and approval.
- Playful fitness. Encourage physical activities that promote play and fun. Games should be simple games—nothing too complicated.
- Variety. String together many of the activities and games in this book.
- Planned activities with you and other family members every day.
- To learn through movement.
- Games and activities that make them feel good about themselves.
- Exploration that allows them to use their curious minds and creative imaginations.
- Activities that help develop their fine and gross motor skills.
- Activities that help build basic fundamental skills and coordination but that aren't beyond their preschool abilities.
- Guidance and direction.
- Rules. Children want to please; they want to know what is right and what is wrong.

To develop endurance, strength, balance, and flexibility, preschoolers need exercises that help them develop a variety of movement skills rather than achieve a high level of movement competence in any one skill.

The National Association for Sport and Physical Education (NASPE) recently issued exercise guidelines recommending that everyone—from babies to toddlers to preschoolers—set aside time for physical activity. Infants need daily activity and should not be confined to a small play space. They should be encouraged to sit, stand, crawl, and walk. Toddlers should have 30 minutes a day of adult-guided activity such as dancing, catching, running, climbing, or chasing. Preschoolers need at least 60 minutes of structured play and at least 60 minutes of unstructured play throughout their day. Preschoolers should not sit for more than 60 minutes at a time, except when sleeping.

 Preschoolers have specific physiological differences that make them unique.

Appropriate Exercises for Preschoolers

When it comes to fitness, kids are not miniature adults. They have specific physiological differences that make them unique. Therefore, their fitness programs, exercises, and activities must be specific to their developmental stage and not just a watered down version of an adult's. The exercises, movements, and games in this book are specifically designed for children who are three to five years old. If you have any concerns regarding physical activities for a child, or if a child has a disability that may limit physical activities, please consult a pediatrician before he participates in any physical activity.

Cardiovascular Exercises

Cardiovascular exercises, also referred to as aerobic activities, are the heart-pumping, heavy-breathing, sweaty-head type of exercises. This type of exercise increases the amount of air or oxygen to the muscles, which helps build endurance. Aerobic activities include walking, running, jumping, skipping, dancing, skating, swimming, and playing games such as basketball or soccer.

Strength Exercises

Preschool-age children do not need resistance equipment to build muscle. They need balance and tumbling exercises to increase their strength.

Flexibility Exercises

Young children are naturally more flexible than older children. Even so, it is important to include flexibility exercises in preschooler exercises to prepare the children's muscles and connective tissue for active games and to get the children into the habit of stretching before any physical activity.

Active Adults Equal Active Kids

Adults play a very important role in children's lives—that of role model. For better or worse, almost everything you say and do is absorbed by your children. Knowing this, you can use your role model status to help your children develop some very positive—and very healthful—habits.

Cognitive Learning

Children are a reflection of their parents and their home environment. Think of preschoolers as sponges: They are absorbing and processing everything you—and the other adults around them—do, everything you say, and the way you say it. They study how you react to certain situations and will remember these reactions and behaviors, especially when a particular action is done repeatedly.

This type of learning is a part of life even in the animal kingdom. Lion cubs aren't born with the skill it takes to hunt prey; they, like our children, learn through cognitive behaviors. The cubs learn to hunt by watching and imitating the behavior of the lioness. Through the lioness's behavior, the cubs learn how to stalk, how to be patient, the time of day to hunt, the type of animal to hunt, and even how to use tall grasses or bushes to conceal themselves. Fortunately we don't have to teach our children to hunt for dinner, but we do teach them attitudes toward life issues, food choices, portion sizes, and active or inactive lifestyles.

 Set the standard for a healthy lifestyle.

As adults and parents, we need to set an example for our children when it comes to healthy eating habits and a regular exercise program. Parents, as well as other family members and adults, automatically become role models for young children. Live by example; inspire your children to take a firm stand by balancing a sedentary lifestyle with an active lifestyle or by replacing unhealthy snacks with healthier choices. What you do—even more than what you say— has an impact on a child.

Ten Healthy Commitments

The list below describes ten commitments that parents should follow to raise healthy children:

1. Be active. The habits that we develop in childhood often stay with us throughout our lives. Exercise and active play need to be at the top of your priority list. Make them a habit and not a chore; they should be as easy to do as brushing your teeth. Sticking with an exercise program requires a lot of hard work and practice, but, in making a commitment to exercise, you are also teaching children discipline, patience, and determination. Arrange for active outings and holidays, play together on weekends, and provide encouragement and support for kids getting involved in sports. Take daily walks or bike rides—do anything but sit. You'll find time for those things that are important to you.

2. Limit "screen time" to encourage more active play. As mentioned, children within this age group should not sit for periods longer than one hour unless they are sleeping. Decide how much time the children should have each day with electronics such as video games, computers, and televisions, and stick to

the rules. Never allow children to eat in front of the television. At home, keep electronics out of children's bedrooms.

3. Introduce healthy foods to children starting at age two. Be sure to choose healthy foods and to read nutrition labels. Feed children a variety of colorful fruits and vegetables. Cut down on snacks and cut out sugary drinks. Pack your own nutritious snacks and meals for outings.

4. Eat dinner as a family, sitting down at the kitchen table, with the television off and conversation on. Now you have ingredient control and portion control.

5. Never use food as a reward or punishment; it puts too much power onto food. Don't say food is "bad" or "good" for you; look at food as fuel to help our bodies operate properly. Never use exercise as a punishment; exercise is something every body needs every day. The children will pick up your attitude toward both food and exercise.

6. Set rules and stick to them! What if a referee decided to change the rules midway through a game? The players would feel confused, and it could become a battle of wills between the referee and players over which rules to follow. Why would anyone want this frustration? Step back and take a look at some of the behaviors that are not contributing to a healthy lifestyle. Then make some changes; add new rules. Rules are not a bad thing; they are guidelines to make life better. It's never too late to bring in a new understanding or rule into the way you run your family; it's just important that you communicate the rules and abide by them. Be a role model. Any change you make in your family lifestyle and behavior will fail if it doesn't start at home.

7. Communicate. Teach children to use words when they are upset or frustrated, not to turn to food or television to forget about their pain. Be sure each child knows that she is loved at any weight, at any fitness level, and at all times. Talk openly about problems, but be careful that your concern isn't interpreted as criticism. Find solutions together and learn from each other. Teach children to believe in themselves and to not set limits on what they can accomplish.

8. Learn a new activity together. As you begin your new healthful lifestyle, learn a new sport or game that will teach your child's body and mind different skills.

9. Designate a room or space for fitness. We have TV rooms, toy rooms, computer rooms, and bedrooms. Why not designate a space in the house for fitness or add a jungle gym in your backyard, with equipment that will encourage physical activity? This room could include mats,

balls, and any other object that will spark children's interest and encourage them to get up and move.

10. Develop a positive attitude. If you find yourself without a positive attitude, refocus your thoughts. In other words, see the bright side of any situation you're facing. We don't have a lot of control over feelings, but we can control our thoughts. Our thoughts are the driving force within us; if we believe our positive thoughts, then we receive the energy we need for today because we believe it will result in producing the end result we are looking for.

Household Chores Are a Physical Activity

To encourage preschoolers to do household chores, make it fun; turn chores into a game. Make a chart and give points for putting clothes away. Add a toy basketball hoop on the hamper so children make a basket every time they throw their dirty socks into it. Create a contest to see who can pick up the most toys, set a timer and record the results.

Recommended Household Chores for Preschool Children

- picking up toys and books
- helping bring laundry to the laundry room
- putting dirty clothes in the hamper
- helping sort laundry (this is a great time to talk about colors)
- wiping up messes (be sure to put paper towels in a place where children can reach them)
- dusting furniture with socks on hands
- helping clear the table
- pulling weeds in the garden
- helping put away groceries
- making beds
- dressing themselves

For the Love of Play

Preschoolers are silly and naturally playful; they take playtime very seriously. To understand our preschoolers, let's look at the world through their eyes. Think of the word *play* as an attitude toward life rather than a form of action. Having a playful attitude toward any activity opens up a world of creative fun.

Preschoolers see life as fun and as an adventure; they see fun in everything from throwing smelly socks at their brother to doing somersaults in the front yard to running through a sprinkler on a summer day. Playtime is good fun for all kids—even kids who are ninety-two years old. Make time for play in your family life, and it will benefit your entire family.

Play is also essential to a child's development because it contributes to the cognitive, physical, social, and emotional well-being of a child. It is even more powerful for a child if family members are involved in active play. Make time for play every day—even on those days when you think you don't have time for fun. Break down the activities into six 10-minute play sessions a day or four 15-minute periods.

Play comes in two basic forms: structured play and unstructured play. Children need a combination of the two forms of play during their day. Adults can take cues from the children as to what activities they find most enjoyable. Be flexible about trying new things.

Structured Play

Structured play is a physical activity taught in a guided environment, with rules, guidelines, and goals. Many parents look to organized sports as a structured way to get their preschoolers active. But the average four-year-old may not have mastered even the basic fundamentals of sports, such as throwing, catching, and following rules. Even simple rules may be hard for them to understand, as any parent who has watched a child run the wrong way during a game knows. And starting any sport too young can be frustrating for kids; it even may discourage a child's future participation in sports. So if you decide to sign up a preschooler for soccer or another team sport, be sure to choose a sport that emphasizes the fundamentals and de-emphasizes winning and keeping score. The American Academy of Pediatrics suggests that team sports are more appropriate for a child six years old and up, while noting that younger children might benefit from a sports class.

Other types of guided play may be better for a preschooler. For example, a softly guided tumbling class is considered structured because it has a few rules to follow (waiting for a turn or using equipment safely) but not so many rules that it makes remembering them difficult. This may be a better way to prepare a child for a more-structured type of lesson in a year or two. The older the preschooler becomes, the more structure you can add to his day. Structured activities can help develop skills that enhance a preschooler's learning.

Preschoolers are old enough to have an opinion when it comes to what they like and don't like. Before you sign up a preschooler for an organized sports team, keep in mind the child's interests. If you think a child will enjoy playing on a soccer team, try out some of the skills it takes for soccer to be sure she will like a particular sport. By selecting an activity that meets all of your criteria, you can help ensure the preschooler will have a positive experience in a structured activity. No matter what the sport or activity, remember that fitness should be fun. If a child isn't having fun, ask why and try to address the issue or find another activity. Listed below are structured activities and lessons that are popular with most preschoolers.

Individual Sports and Activities

- bowling
- croquet
- cross-country skiing
- downhill skiing
- floor exercises
- Frisbee
- gymnastics
- ice skating
- Pilates
- swimming
- tumbling
- yoga
- dance (This includes many types of dance, such as ballet, hip hop, interpretive, jazz, modern, tap)
- martial arts (*martial* means "fighting," but it is an art form that has become a sport. Martial arts are rich in tradition; they require discipline and strength from the mind and body.)

Team Sports

- basketball
- golf
- soccer
- softball
- T-ball (baseball)
- tennis

Unstructured, or Free, Play

Kids at this age can't seem to sit still. Their minds are always thinking, and their bodies are always moving. This is an important stage of discovery. Support this stage and direct the energy in a positive way to take advantage of your child's natural tendency to be active with free play. Unstructured play is vital to a child's physical and mental development. Unstructured play has no rules or directions to follow; it has only the creative limits of a child's imagination. Unstructured play is a powerful activity for all preschoolers because it develops intellect and emotional and social skills.

The American Academy of Pediatrics recommends that toddlers and preschoolers not sit for longer than 30 minutes and 60 minutes, respectively, at a time. Yet, within the last 30 years, American children have increased the amount of time they are sedentary (playing video and computer games and watching television) and decreased the amount of time they are active with creative play. So if moving toward unstructured play is new for children, they initially may resist the change, even claiming boredom. But just remember: From boredom, creativity is born.

It is important that parents and other involved adults take an active roll behind the scenes to allow children to have creative play. Because it is unstructured, this playtime can be as simple as you want. It can be a child imaginatively playing by himself or with a friend, parent, or teacher; it can be enjoyed either inside or outside. Encourage the children's active play by setting up a play area or playroom with equipment such as a low basketball hoop or a soft mat for gymnastics. If you stock it with balls or other equipment, make sure everything is within the preschoolers' reach.

At times, preschoolers want and need adults to be involved in their world of play. When you or other adults spend time with children at play, it gives importance to their play and helps build their self-esteem. To make the most of your playtime together, think like a kid and use your imagination along with your child's imagination. How would Superman kick this ball? Now how would a Barbie doll kick this ball? How would Sleeping Beauty kick this ball? Even watching them play is beneficial; it shows you support this time with them.

Many everyday interactions can be turned into play. For example, you can use imaginative or thematic play by reading your child's favorite book with them and then acting out the scenes together. You can also video record your child's interpretation of a story such as *The Three Little Pigs*. Such ideas are limited only by your imagination.

Let the World Be Your Gym

Just as with imaginative play, active play is limited only by your imagination. Maybe you and your preschoolers would enjoy a weekend afternoon of physical activities at a local community center. Explore other opportunities that your community may provide, such as holiday parades, ethnic festivals, historical walks, or cycling tour of your town. Even playgrounds, swing sets, and homemade forts are treasure troves of fun and active free playtime! Walk or bike to a nearby playground, challenge children to try their skills swinging on swings or crossing a horizontal ladder. To encourage more physical activity at the playground, bring a bag packed with toys to encourage additional play. Some items to bring might include books, bubbles, pails, a jump rope, balls, and sidewalk chalk.

Simple options, such as taking a hike with preschoolers, can be lots of fun. A hike is a good way of combining exploration and exercise. It's also a great time to teach children to appreciate the outdoors. But before you start your mountain trek with a three-year-old in tow, do your homework. Most preschoolers can hike anywhere from one to two miles but will need frequent breaks along the route. Research your local parks to determine if they are kid friendly. Do they have bathrooms? Do they include child-friendly trails? Are there interesting sites for your preschooler to see like creeks, waterfalls, or open fields?

Being prepared will ensure success for your outing. Choose a time of the day that won't be too hot and won't interfere with a child's nap time. Be sure the children wear appropriate clothing. And in addition to a bag of appropriate toys—such as a pail and shovel for digging and a magnifying glass for exploring—pack sunscreen and bug repellent. Bring along a blanket for resting and pack a picnic lunch with plenty of fluids. Also bring a camera for taking pictures. If you keep in mind that the hike is intended for preschoolers and plan it with their needs and endurance level in mind, everyone will have a good time.

Learning Through Play

Through play, preschoolers learn about life and the world around them. Games and sports allow them to experience the consequences of their actions and will teach specific values, some of which will stay with them for the rest of their lives.

Physical Skills Teach Competence

Teaching children new skills can build confidence both physically and mentally. Young children need to develop competence in movement skills; simple movements become the building blocks for more complex movements. Start with a basic skill level and encourage children to feel competent along their development before adding a new skill. If you see a child is struggling, go back to the skill level before the current one and work on that skill until everyone feels they have mastered it. Only then will you want to move to the next level. Our job is to nurture that "I can do anything" belief.

Kids actually want to be their best. So to motivate children to be competent, give praise for a job well done or offer encouragement when they feel they could have done better. Let a child hear she did a great job and how wonderful she is. Be specific with praise and encouragement, such as, "I am so impressed that you caught that ball." Be sure to give praise in the moment, and you also can repeat it later when other people, especially family members, are around. A smile, a thumbs up, or a pat on the back is sometimes all it takes to show your support for a preschooler's new skill.

Play Builds Mental Skills

Teaching children about relationships may not be something you would think about when playing games, but it is a great opportunity to develop social skills such as sharing, controlling emotions, showing respect, and supporting teammates. Playing games can have very practical goals: Play a name game to introduce one child to another or use game rules to reinforce listening skills, making sure that all children listen when one child has a question.

Emotionally and socially, children of this age are beginning to manage their feelings, and games present all sorts of opportunities to explore them. If a child has a temper when a game doesn't go his way, discuss good sportsmanship. Comment when you see children playing nicely together. Children at this age get embarrassed easily; if you see this happen, help them feel more confident in their abilities. And if you or other adults are playing games with the children, don't cheat to let them win. It's okay to let kids fail. I am not suggesting that you slam dunk shots over a five-year-old's head; I'm suggesting you don't purposely lose because you don't want the children to feel bad. Children must experience winning without bragging and losing without crying or having a temper tantrum.

Although competition will come into play as children grow older, it should not be used with this age group unless you're playfully challenging a child. By teaching children this soft approach to competition, you are sending the message that competition is a way for children to challenge themselves and to work as a team. The goal is not to win or lose; it is to do our best. Consider games with this age group as an introduction to competition. For instance, a two-year-old will not enjoy a relay race, but she may enjoy a lesser level of competition if an adult makes it fun. For example, you might say, "Watch me jump. Can you jump higher?" Or you might say to a four-year-old, "I think I can do five jumping jacks. How many can you do?" With preschoolers, avoid games in which players are eliminated. Children at this age do not want to sit quietly on the sideline watching the other children play a game. And recognize each child for his strengths, but don't compare one child to another. Comparison may create negative feelings and animosity in children.

Learning New Games Teaches Focus

Teaching a child how to play a new game can be challenging. Most preschool-age children have short attention spans, so as adults we must be creative. First connect before you direct: Ask all the kids to look you in the eyes and then talk to them. The games that work best for this age group are those that have only a few, simple directions to follow and give only one task at a time. Stay brief, stay simple, and have the kids repeat directions back to you. Ask questions to be sure they are listening.

Playful Activities Teach Sharing

Sharing can be a difficult task for a preschooler to learn, mainly because up until this age she wasn't expected to share anything. Learning how to share feels good. To encourage the idea that sharing is fun, talk to your preschooler before friends come for a visit. If there is a special toy that your child does not want to share, put it away during this playtime. Then ask your child what toys she would like to share. Explain that you share things with your friends and that sharing makes everybody happy. And—especially important to a pre-schooler—explain that our friends do not keep the things we share with them; they will give the toys back. Introduce sharing to larger groups of children by turning sharing into a game. For example, working with a puzzle, have each child pick a piece. Then taking turns, each child contributes his piece to the group puzzle.

Games and Sports Encourage Thinking

Children of this age group begin to think through situations. Games and exercises can be used to develop that skill. Consider the game "Reverse Simon Says," in which players listen and do the reverse of what Simon says. Other thinking games can build on what preschoolers already enjoy, such as letters, counting, and colors. Have them use their imagination to stretch their bodies to form the letter A... or perform Jumping Jacks (#173) while yelling out different colors. Other active games can teach children to make decisions. For example, "Follow the Leader" (#163) teaches children to make a decision, act it out, and watch how others follow their lead.

For added fun and encouragement for your preschool players, you might allow older children to teach younger children how to play a game.

Where to Start for Parents, Teachers, Coaches, and Counselors

The exercises described in this book have been kid approved. In other words, kids simply enjoy them, as I have discovered in using them for personal training sessions, kid fitness classes, kid fitness camps, birthday parties, and in schools. Reading through them, you may think some of the activities seem silly; others may seem too easy. But, remember, these exercises are for preschoolers. The movements they incorporate were designed for preschool muscles and coordination.

How to Use the Preschooler-Approved Exercises

Each of these exercises and games was created with children. Children love to be silly, creative, and imaginative, and they also love to see you enjoying this time with them. So to receive the most enjoyment out of each exercise and game, you must think like a kid, have fun, and enjoy the workout.

But before you jump into it, below are a few considerations for you as the leader.

Consider Safety First

Safety is a number-one concern when working with children and exercise. Most important, children need supervision in any activity. Beyond that, be sure that the area in which you have the children playing is free of electrical cords, sharp objects, or anything that may harm children. And if equipment is needed, be sure it is age appropriate and that the children know how to use each piece correctly. Use safety equipment such as helmets and pads if the sport calls for it. Make sure the children dress in appropriate clothing for the weather and, even in cooler temperatures, keep them hydrated. When outside, sunscreen is always a must.

Review Each Section Heading

Within each section, you will find level notations: The levels run from level one, the easiest, up to level 10, which is the most challenging. Preschool children are visual learners; demonstrate each activity before you teach them how to perform it. It is very important to start with level one; perform the activity until the children feel as if they have mastered the movement. Then move on to level two and so on up to level ten. Each level builds on the previous level, by adding a new technique, speed, travel movement, or additional skill. Remember: The goal is for children to feel competent with the action or movement before moving on to the next level of skill.

Be a Teacher

The following steps can be used to teach children anything from how to make a bed to how to play flashlight tag, or how to perform a particular skill. All children learn at different rates, so you may have to spend more time on one step than on others. Or you may have to go back and review a step before moving on to the next step.

Note: Sitting and Standing Exercises

Unless otherwise designated, participants can either sit in a chair or stand, and should keep feet hip-distance apart. If the exercises call for sitting on a chair, children's feet should touch the ground. For shorter children whose feet are unable to reach the floor, add a stack of books. Each participant's hands should rest on his thighs or at the side of his body."

Step 1: Demonstrate to your preschoolers how to do or play a particular activity. Explain why you want it done this way. Be sure to ask if they have questions.

Step 2: Have your preschoolers do the activity with you. Review the reasons for performing the activity, chore, or game in this manner. Be sure to praise them.

Step 3: Have your preschoolers do the activity alone, while you watch them. If something is left out or the chore is not done properly, now is the time to review the steps again.

Step 4: Have your preschoolers do the activity, or chore all by themselves, without you being by their side. Be sure to praise a job well done!

Promote Good Health and Skill Building as Fun

Remember: Kids want to have fun. What follows is how 75,000 kids and I have made exercising fun.

Partner Training

What better way is there to spend quality time with your preschoolers and exercise at the same time? An adult can participate with a preschooler or select another preschooler to be a partner and choose a group of exercises and enjoy some active play.

Personal Training

In the beginning, introduce children to these exercises/movements one at a time. Be sure to read the description thoroughly, and, eventually, children will become familiar with them. Choose five exercises per day and then replace them with five new exercises the following day.

Exercise Stations

This exercise format combines many exercises in one workout. It can be used for 1 or 100 players. Decide on a theme that your preschoolers would enjoy. Some themes they may have fun with include:

- animal stations
- baseball stations
- healthy-heart stations
- soccer stations
- stations that use only balls

Read through the book and choose eight to ten different exercises—one for each station. Be sure to include all components of fitness: stretching, balance, aerobic, tumbling, and skill performance. Write the name for each exercise and its description on a card. Include either the number of repetitions for each exercise or the time allowance for each station on the card, too. Put all of the station cards in a circle large enough so that the players can move from one station to another and have plenty of workout space. On "Go," each person chooses a station and stands in front of the card there. (Typically I suggest that only one person is at each station, but preschoolers may want to work in pairs.) Participants complete the exercises at each station for one complete cycle; allow those who want to, to do it all over again.

Interval Training

Add a cardiovascular activity in between each station. Have children perform the cardio exercise for a set period of time (for example, 1 minute) and then move to the next station.

For example, choose from:

- hopping on one leg
- jumping
- kicking (forward, backward, and side to side)
- running (forward, backward, sideways)

Scavenger Hunt

A scavenger hunt is a game in which you prepare a list of specific objects to find and the players then gather or capture the objects in a photograph. Scavenger hunts can be played indoors or outdoors. You can make any hike, stroll through the park, or walk in the mall on a rainy day more fun if you prepare a list of treasures to find. A hunt is a great way to teach kids about specific topics, such as architecture, or history, or nature. Be sure to record their findings.

Obstacle Course

Create an obstacle course by choosing a series of exercises from this book and then writing the title and description of each on a separate card. Place the cards around a good-sized room, creating a free-for-all obstacle course. Remove unsafe objects from the room (tables with sharp edges, for example) and clear out any clutter that could trip someone. Then place piles of cushions, sturdy chairs, laundry baskets, or other items around the room for the kids to romp over, under, or through on their way to the exercise cards. A large cardboard box, if you have one, can make an excellent tunnel. Players must navigate their way through the challenging series of exercises. Timing is optional.

Relay Races

With the children, designate the starting line and the finish line of a racecourse. Choose from any of the activities listed in this book. Demonstrate the activity's movement to be sure all children understand the exercise. Remember children of this age do not like competition, so be sure to emphasize the fun and not winning or losing.

A Theme of a Book

Select a storybook to read to your preschooler and then select a list of exercises from this book that would fit the storybook's theme. For example, if the book you are reading is about animals, choose animal exercises to perform.

Backward Activities

Choose a list of movements and perform all of the activities backward. This one is best for older preschool children.

Stuffed-Animal Exercises

Invite children to choose a favorite stuffed animal and have the animal "play along" on each activity.

Theme Day

Choose a theme and have children wear a costume that represents that theme. This is extra fun when the adults dress up to do the exercises, too.

Pyramid Style

Select ten to fifteen exercises from the book, and write each exercise on a single card. Perform the exercise on one card, pick a second card, perform that particular exercise, and then repeat card one. Continue to add on a new card and repeat each of the previous exercises until you have completed all of the cards.

Choreograph

Select a style of music your children will enjoy. Slow songs work well with ballet, country, or ballroom dance movements; pop music works well with faster movements. Compile a list of eight to ten exercises or movements from the book that would work well with your chosen style and song. Link one movement together with the next movement until you have a choreographed dance routine.

Vacation

If your family is planning a trip around some outdoor adventure such as skiing, kayaking, hiking, or swimming, use that activity as your theme. Then choose exercises and games that will help prepare the muscles that will be used during your adventure. Be sure to take along this book to keep your family in shape while you travel.

Visit a Ball Game or Soccer Game

Taking young children to a ball game can be very exciting. You can increase the excitement by focusing on the skills needed for those particular sports, before and after the visit to the game. Practice some of the drills listed in this book. Let the children see how the exercises they have been doing apply to the ball game.

Birthday-Party Games

Any of the exercises or active games in this book can be fun for use at birthday parties.

Create a Game Plan

Preschool-age children have very short attention spans, so be prepared with many activities for them to do. When planning any exercise program, choose a group of activities that start off slow and gradually become more physically challenging before slowing down in pace once more. Look at the activities that you have planned and place them in order of energy expenditure. Start off with activities that will get the children moving but won't exhaust their energy levels from the beginning. Next add on another activity that requires more energy, and for the peak of the bell-shaped curve, plot the activity with the highest level of energy expenditure. After that, gradually decrease the energy level of the activities until it is time for the children to cool down. End the session with some cool-down stretches.

Here are some examples of game plans. This list of activities takes approximately 30 to 45 minutes to complete. For any of the programs, gather any equipment you will need before you begin.

Example Number One (*30 minutes*)

1. Play "Head, Shoulders, Knees, and Toes" (song game).

2. Play Simon Says (#31): I use this game to get children to stretch and walk around the room to warm up their muscles.

3. Imitate animal movements: Create a game that lets children imitate animal movements by choosing a combination of 10 animals to mimic.

4. Do three Jumping Skills: Choose three of the skills listed (#166–#177).

5. Do Relay Races (#156).

6. Choose a combination of 5 to 10 exercises from the games list to create an obstacle course (see page vi).

7. Choose 3 strength-building exercises (#33–#76).

8. Choose 3 balance activities (#134–#142) or the Statue game (#145).

9. Play Follow the Leader (#163).

10. Play the Graveyard Game (#32): Use this for a cool down.

Example Number Two (*30 Minutes*)

1. Play "Head, Shoulders, Knees, and Toes."

2. Choose 5 stretches (#5–#30).

3. Choose 5 strength-building exercises (#33–#76).

4. Choose 1 fine motor skill (#127–#133).

5. Play Freeze Tag (#144).

6. Play the "Hokey Pokey."

Example Number Three (*30 minutes*)

1. Play "The Wheels on the Bus."

2. Play the Popcorn Game (#2).

3. Choose 5 stretches (#5–#30).

4. Choose 5 strength-building exercises (#33–#76).

5. Choose 3 running games (#146–#165).

6. Choose 3 rhythm games (#279–#303).

Games to Avoid

- games that are above children's skill levels
- games that are too competitive
- games that are too complicated for this age group

- games that could potentially hurt children
- games that end with a winner and a loser
- elimination games

Exercising in Hot or Cold Weather

During hot weather, it's important to prevent children from getting over-heated and dehydrated. Young children are in more danger of both for several reasons. They have a greater surface-area-to-body-mass ratio than adults, so they absorb more heat from the sun and air. On a cold day, they have a greater heat loss than adults. Because they don't sweat as much as adults, they produce more heat, so they don't cool off as well. Kids take playing games very seriously so they aren't aware that they need to take a break and drink some water. Children with certain medical conditions, including obesity, diabetes, or heart disease, are at even greater risk for overheating and dehydration.

For these reasons, it is better to postpone or reschedule strenuous activity when heat and humidity are high. Even under more normal conditions, always make sure that preschoolers are taking in plenty of fluids before, during, and after exercise. Have them drink 4 to 8 ounces of liquid 30 minutes before an activity. Then, every 20 to 30 minutes during the activity, give them another 4 to 8 ounces, and, finally, after the activity, have everyone drink another 4 to 8 ounces of water. On especially hot and humid days, have children spend as much time indoors as possible. If your home does not have air conditioning, go to a public place like a shopping mall to walk around. Also have the children avoid too much sunshine. Instead, slow their activities and have them play in the shade. On such days, everyone should wear lightweight clothing, including a hat, apply sunscreen, and take a cool bath or shower. Try using a spray mister to cool down active children.

Recommended Equipment

Many children of this age begin playing organized sports such as basketball, T-ball, soccer, gymnastics, martial arts, hockey, and dance. This may be an age of discovery, but it's also one of new sports, adventures, and especially new equipment. The following recommended equipment, though not a complete list, is a good starting point to enhance gross- and fine-motor skills and to encourage children to become more active:

- balloons
- balls in a variety of shapes and sizes
- basketball hoop (size appropriate)
- beanbags

- chairs
- child's size golf clubs (plastic is good)
- clothespins
- colored feathers (can be purchased at a crafts shop)
- cotton balls
- croquet sets
- DVDs—dance and fitness
- elbow pads
- empty plastic bottles
- Frisbees
- garden tools
- hacky sack
- helmets
- hula hoops, in a variety of sizes
- jump ropes, including the Chinese jump rope
- kickboards and swimming toys
- matchbox cars (or other cars with wheels)
- mini tennis rackets
- nets for kicking and throwing balls
- parachutes or big blankets
- pedometers
- Ping-Pong paddle and balls
- plastic golf set
- resistance bands
- safety cones (of different colors; for setting boundaries)
- scarves
- scooter
- sidewalk chalk for games
- skates
- stopwatches
- straws
- swimming equipment
- swing set
- tents

- trampolines
- tricycles
- T-ball stand
- tunnels
- water balloons
- whiffle balls
- whistles
- yoga mats

The key to getting kids to exercise is capturing their imaginations so that they see participating as fun.

Key to the Icons Used in the Games

To help you find games suitable for a particular situation, the games included in this book are coded with symbols or icons. These icons tell you, at a glance, the following details about the game:

- the size of the group needed
- if a large space is needed
- if physical contact is or might be involved
- if participants will exercise on a mat
- if props are required
- if music is required

These icons are explained in more detail below. Two of the icons included in other SmartFun books—those for "age level" and "time"—have been omitted here because the games presented here are categorized by skill level rather than age level and because the duration of each game will vary depending on a number of factors, including the size of the group, the physical activity involved, the time limit set by the leader, variations or modifications made by the leader, and whether the particular game appeals to the players.

The size of the group needed. Most of the activities may be performed with groups of any size. A few are designed for pairs, small groups, or the whole group. These exceptions are individually marked with one of the following group-size icons:

 = The whole group plays together.

 = Participants play individually, so any size group can play.

= Participants play in small groups of three or more.

 = Participants play in pairs.

If a large space is needed. A large space is required for a few of the games, such as when the whole group is required to form a circle or to walk around the room. These games are marked with the following icon:

 = The exercise may require a larger space.

If physical contact is or might be involved. Although a certain amount of body contact might be acceptable in certain environments, the following icon has been inserted at the top of any games that definitely involves contact or might involve anything from a small amount of contact to minor collisions. You can figure out in advance if the game is suitable for your participants and/ or environment.

 = Physical contact is involved or likely.

If an exercise mat is required. Many of the exercises in this book should be done on an exercise mat.

 = Players will exercise on mats.

If props are required. Many of the games require no special props. In some cases, though, items such as balls, jump ropes, chairs, or other materials are integral to playing a game. Games requiring props are flagged with the icon below, and the necessary materials are listed under the Props heading. Note that optional props will also be flagged.

= Props are needed.

If music is required. Only a few games in this book require recorded music. If the music is optional, it is noted as such; if it is required, the icon below is used:

 = Music is required.

The Exercises and Games

Sing-Along and Movement Games

Sing-along and movement games are an excellent way to get preschoolers to move to music. They are a fun way to integrate warming up the body, motor skills, coordination, discussion of body parts, body awareness, and thinking skills all rolled up in to a fun song and dance. These familiar songs and dances are not included in the List of Games. However, you may want to refer to this section when you are looking for a warm-up or a cool-down activity:

- "Head, Shoulders, Knees, and Toes"
- "I'm a Little Teapot"
- "Wheels on the Bus"
- "Hokey Pokey"
- "Looby Loo"
- "Row, Row, Row Your Boat"

Basic Exercises: Let the Fun Begin!

Preschoolers are naturally playful; they just want to have fun. Preschoolers have short attention spans, so a good basic rule for the following games and activities is to let the preschoolers perform the movement 10 times, unless otherwise specified. Make sure that each child is properly supervised during the performance of each activity or movement for their own safety.

 Fun is the secret to getting kids to do almost anything.

Active Games for Warm-Up

any size
Except as noted

Warm-up activities do more than prepare the heart and muscles for the exercises ahead, they also set the tone and energy levels for more strenuous exercise and teach children good physical education habits. Encourage children to warm up with fun games in which everyone will want to participate.

 ## Spell It Out

small groups

This game requires children to think about letters, spelling, and how to move their bodies creatively. If you are playing this game for the first time, demonstrate how to create letters of the alphabet using your body.

Tell the children: Practice creating letters of the alphabet with your bodies. You can make letters by yourself or with a partner. Once you have done this a few times, put some of the letters together to spell a word. Try some simple words such as cat or ball.

Tip Words that work well are small words such as *ball, cat, sun…*

Popcorn Game

This is a quick and fun game to get the kids' heart rates up. Have them act out the story as you recite it to them. Demonstrating the motions as you speak will help them.

Tell the children: I'm going to tell you a story that we can act out together. First I will say, "I'm a piece of popcorn. Put me in a pot. Shake me as fast as you can." As I do, we all pretend we are a piece of popcorn and shimmy and jump down to the ground. Then I'll say, "When I get hot enough, up I pop!" and we'll jump up as high as we can.

The Waltz

Music To allow the kids to hear the 3/4 beat or one chord per measure, play "The Blue Danube" by Johann Strauss or "Valses Sentimentales" by Franz Shubert. For more current music, you could play "Come Away with Me" by Norah Jones, "Open Arms" by Journey, "Kiss from a Rose" by Seal, or "How Can I Be Sure" by the Rascals.

The waltz, with its fluid movements, is a great way to get kids warmed up, and this game teaches preschoolers the basic steps to the waltz. The kids do not need partners; just have them learn the footwork on their own.

Tell the children: The waltz pattern resembles a box. It can be broken down into two half boxes—a forward half box and a backward half box. Each half box includes three steps. For the forward half box: (1) Step forward left foot. (2) Right foot moves to the side, and (3) left foot closes to right foot. For the backward half box: (1) Right foot moves back. (2) Left foot moves to the side, and (3) right foot closes to left foot.

Goin' Crazy

This was a favorite activity with my preschool children. Believe me: They know what going crazy means. Anything goes, and it's a fun way to wake up the muscles and get the kids laughing. Repeat this activity for 3 minutes.

Tell the children: Go crazy. Anything goes!

Stretching Exercises

any size

Except as noted

Demonstrate an exercise first.
Then teach the children how to perform it.

Stretching is good for any body: It helps prepare the muscles, tendons, and ligaments for an activity and helps prevent injuries. Your body recovers better after an exercise if you stretch. Perform each stretching activity. Hold each position and have your preschoolers count to 10.

Upper Body

All of the muscles in our bodies are meant to work together. Upper-body movement requires a tightened core to keep balance and form, good posture is necessary to prevent back pain and maintain proper form in most sports, and upper-body strength allows us to maintain balance and move at a faster pace.

Neck Rolls

First demonstrate the movement.

Tell the children: Drop your chin to your chest. Slowly roll your head from one side to the other. Repeat this movement 2 times.

Shoulder Lifts

Tell the children: Squeeze and lift your shoulders up to your earlobes. Breathe and hold for 10 seconds. Slowly allow your shoulders to relax to the starting position. Repeat this movement 5 times.

Variation To work on coordination, ask the children to perform this stretch one shoulder at a time.

Arm Circles

Tell the children: Stretch your arms out at your sides, shoulder height. Begin circling your arms in one direction 5 times. Reverse the circle and go in the opposite direction. Repeat this movement 5 times. Create big circles and little circles.

Front-of-the-Shoulder Stretch

Tell the children: In a standing position, bring both hands behind your back and try to interlace your fingers. Breathe and hold this position for 10 seconds.

Back-of-the-Shoulder Stretch

Tell the children: Reach your right arm straight in front of you. Bend your left arm and put your left wrist on the back of your right arm, just above the elbow. Use your left arm to gently press the right arm across the body. Hold for 10 to 30 seconds and then switch to the other arm.

Triceps Stretch

This stretch works the triceps, the muscle on the back of the upper arm.

Tell the children: Raise your right arm straight up overhead. Then bend your elbow so the fingers touch or reach toward the middle of your upper back. Grab your right elbow with your left hand. Pull gently until you feel the stretch in your right arm. Hold for 10 to 30 seconds and then switch to the other arm.

Our lower-body muscles are the biggest muscles in our bodies. We use these muscles primarily for movement, so it is important to include lower-body-strengthening exercises no matter what our fitness goals or age. Lower-body-strengthening exercises help to increase strength and endurance, aid in weight loss, and can improve posture as well.

Butterfly Wings

Tell the children: In a seated position with your knees pointing to each side, bring the bottoms of your feet together. Hold your feet with your hands. Slowly raise and lower your knees 5 times.

Smell Your Stinky Toes

Tell the children: In a seated position with your knees pointing to each side, bring the bottoms of your feet together. Hold your feet with your hands and then lean over from your waist, trying to touch your nose to your toes. Hold and count to 10.

Row, Row, Row Your Boat

Divide the group into pairs or have the players choose partners.

Tell the children: Sit on the floor facing your partner with your legs spread apart and your feet touching your partner's feet. Grasp hands. One partner leans back as if "rowing a boat" and then pulls upright to sit. Then the other partner takes a turn and starts by leaning back. You can take turns and sing "Row, Row, Row Your Boat" to make it more enjoyable.

Tip If the pair is comprised of an adult and a child, the adult sits on floor with her legs apart. The child sits opposite with his legs on the inside of the adult's.

Leg Stretch

Tell the children: Start with your feet about shoulder-width apart and your hands on your hips. Take a giant step forward with one leg. Bending both knees, lower yourself as far as you can without losing balance. Hold for 1 or 2 seconds, keeping your torso straight and making sure your weight is on your front leg and not on the knee as you hold, and then raise yourself up using your upper-leg muscles, stepping backward to your original starting position. Repeat this stretch 6 to 8 times on one leg and then change legs, or do the repetitions alternating legs.

Straddle Stretch

Tell the children: Sit with your legs apart in what is called a straddle position. *Be sure to use the term* straddle *in this and other straddle exercises so the children become familiar with the word.* Twist your torso toward your right leg and bend forward over that leg until you feel a stretch. Hold the stretch for 10 seconds without bouncing, and then return to an upright sitting position and repeat the exercise with your left leg.

16 Quadriceps Stretch

Props A chair or countertop

Tell the children: Stand facing the back of a chair or a counter. Using your left arm for balance, bend your right leg behind you and grab it with your right hand. Gently pull your foot toward your bottom until you feel the stretch in the front of your thigh. Breathe, hold for 10 seconds, and then switch legs.

17 Walk on Toes

Tell the children: Walk on your tippy toes and count to 30.

18 Walk on Heels

This may be difficult for preschool children to master.
Tell the children: Walk on the heels of your feet and count to 30.

19 Calf Stretch

Props A wall or countertop

Tell the children: Place your hands on a wall or countertop. Stand with right leg near the wall. Take a giant step backward with your left foot; do not bend your knees and keep both heels on the floor. You should feel a stretch in the calf muscle of your left leg. Breathe and hold without bouncing for 10 seconds. Repeat with your other leg.

20 Inner-Thigh Stretch

Tell the children: Stand up straight with your legs a little farther than shoulder-width apart and your toes and heels on the floor pointing out at about a

45-degree angle. Bend your right knee to a 90-degree angle but keep your right knee over your right ankle. Keep your left leg stretched out straight. Breathe and hold the stretch for 10 seconds, and then switch legs.

 ## 21 Back-of-the-Leg Stretch

Tell the children: Stand with your arms at your sides and your feet together. Bending forward, roll your back down, reaching for your toes with your hands. Hold this stretch for 5 seconds and then slowly return to a standing position. Repeat this stretch 2 times. Be sure not to bounce.

Chest and back exercises help to develop the core muscles and improve posture.

 ## 22 Hug Yourself

It is great to do this exercise every day!

Tell the children: Wrap your arms around yourself and give yourself a big hug. Do this for 10 seconds.

 ## 23 Knee to Chest

Tell the children: Lie on your back, knees up, with both feet flat on the floor. Bring your left knee into your chest and give it a hug. Hold and count to 10. Place this foot on the floor and repeat the exercise with your other leg.

Elephant Stretch

Tell the children: In a standing position, lace your fingers together in front of your body and bend over slowly. Bend forward until your back is straight and parallel to the ground, and then swing your arms back and forth like an elephant's trunk as you walk forward. Do this movement for 10 seconds.

Swan Stretch

This exercise stretches the chest.

Tell the children: Kneel on the ground on your hands and knees and then bring your feet under your hips so you can sit back on your heels while keeping your back straight. Push your back backward, and as you do so, allow your arms to come forward. Then reverse the movement, pulling your back forward and allowing your arms to go behind your back. Hold each stretch for 15 seconds.

Superman Stretch

Tell the children: In a standing position, place your hands on your hips and pull your shoulders back as far as they will go. You should feel a stretch in your chest. Hold this stretch for 30 seconds.

Seal

Tell the children: Sit back almost on your heels. Point your hands to the side and place them on the floor for balance. Lift your chest to straighten your elbows. Keep your bottom off of your heels. Hold the pose for 10 seconds and breathe.

28 Cat and Cow

Tell the children: Stand with feet hip-width apart. Next, bend over and place your hands right above your knees. Round your back upward toward the sky and pull your belly button in toward your spine. Hold this position for 10 seconds. Release your back to sag slightly and stretch your back in the opposite direction. Hold this position for 10 seconds.

29 Overhead

Tell the children: In a standing position, extend your arms up and over your head, holding your hands together. Pretend you are reaching for something that is a little out of your reach. Repeat this exercise for 10 seconds.

30 Full-Body Stretch

Tell the children: Lie on your back with your legs extended. Stretch both arms overhead. Pretend as if someone is pulling your arms in one direction and your feet in another. Hold this stretch for 30 seconds.

Active Games

Games are a great way to involve all kids in being active. Some kids will play as much as they can, while others may need a little more encouragement to get started. Find ways to make sure that everyone is able to participate.

31 Simon Says

whole group

This game is a great listening game. And it is especially wonderful because you can turn the game into any activity you wish. Simon Says can be used for warm-ups, stretching, cardiovascular exercise, or relaxing time. You can use it when asking a child to do chores, and you can use it just about anywhere: in the grocery store, at grandma's house, in the car, and more. Choose one person to be Simon. The game usually works best when an adult is Simon first.

Tell the children: The person who is Simon will give directions. Simon may say, "Simon says jump up and down" or "Simon says tap your head." Everyone should do the movement Simon says—as long as he says, "Simon says." But if Simon gives a direction without saying "Simon says," don't do it. If Simon says, "Stand on one leg" but doesn't say, "Simon says," anyone who stands on one leg must sit out one turn.

Tip When playing with children of this age, you don't want to eliminate any players.

32 Graveyard Game

whole group

This game is fun for families and groups and is best played in groups of three or more. You can use it as a cool-down game, especially when you want kids to calm down. This game is best played in low lighting or with no lights at all. Play this game for 5–7 minutes to cool the kids down.

Tell the children: In this game, one person is the graveyard keeper; everyone else lies on the floor. Players must lie perfectly still on the floor when the gravedigger passes. Try not to laugh when she moves your body into funny positions.

Exercises to Build Strong Muscles

Demonstrate an exercise first.
Then teach the children how to perform it.

Children at this age will be using their body weight as resistance while enjoying muscle-strengthening activities in a gamelike environment. Use simple directions coupled with visual demonstration to increase players' understanding. These exercises are not divided into categories because most of the exercises are muscle building for the entire body at once. The following exercises are fun for every member of a family and for people of all ages.

 ## Wall Push-Ups

Props A wall

Wall Push-Ups are a great way to teach someone how to master a push-up.

Tell the children: Stand about an arm's distance away from a wall with your legs together. Place your hands on the wall just a little wider than your shoulders. Lean forward and touch your nose to the wall and then push back to the starting position. Make sure to keep your body in a straight line with your heels on the floor. Repeat this exercise for 1 minute.

 ## Wheelbarrow

pairs

Letting the kids take turns being the wheelbarrow makes for a fun game, but it requires some upper-body strength. Divide the group into pairs or have the players choose partners.

Tell the children: Have your partner lie face down on the floor. Stand between his feet, facing his head, and grasp his ankles. Keeping his hands on the floor, he will push up with his arms until they are straight, and you will lift his ankles until you are standing straight and holding his ankles at your sides. Then, with head up, he will walk on his hands forward 20 steps while you walk forward and support his body and he tries not to let it sag. When you are finished, switch roles.

 ## Bear Crawl

Tell the children: On your hands and knees, crawl along the floor keeping yourself low to the ground but keeping your chest off the floor. Move around the space trying not to hop but to run on all fours. Repeat this movement for 3 minutes.

Variation The exercise can be done moving forward, backward, or sideways.

 ## Twist and Build

Props Blocks (or other small objects) for each participant

Place a set of blocks or a quantity of any item that a child can easily grasp on the floor. Have the child sit on the floor, legs straight, with the blocks piled on one side of the child's hips.

    Tell the children: On the word "Go," rotate your upper body only. Pick up one block at a time and place it down next to your other hip. Repeat this until all the blocks are moved from one side to the other. Be sure to repeat the movement from the other side. Repeat this exercise for 2 minutes.

 ## Imaginary Bicycle

Tell the children: Lie on your back with your feet up in the air. Pedal your feet as if you are pedaling a bicycle. Repeat this movement for 3 minutes.

Variation Instruct the children to go fast, slow, backward, and wide-legged.

Step on That Bug

This is a lunge exercise, but kids will know what to do if you tell them to step on a bug.

Tell the children: With your hands on your hips, take a giant step forward with your right foot, bending your right knee to a 90-degree angle. As you bend your knee, make sure your it does not go farther forward than the tip of your shoe. Return to the starting position and repeat the exercise with your other leg. Repeat this exercise for 3 minutes.

Variation Point in the direction in which you want the children to "step on the bug"—sideways, on a diagonal, etc. Mix it up and make it fun.

"Motor Cross" Speedway

Props A pair of toy cars with wheels (like Hot Wheels cars) for each participant

Tell the children: Lie on your back with your knees bent. Hold a car in each hand and place the cars on your thighs. Curl your upper body up and push the cars to the tops of your knees. Roll the cars all the way down your leg until you reach your toes. Reverse the cars, rolling them all the way up to your knees, and then lie back down and bring the cars back to the top of your thighs. Repeat this exercise 5 times.

Snake in the Grass

Tell the children: Lie on your stomach with your palms touching the floor next to your shoulders. Push your chest off the ground and hiss like a snake twice. Then lower your chest back to the ground. Repeat this exercise 5 times.

Bridge

Tell the children: Lie on your back with your knees bent and the bottoms of your feet on the floor. Lift your hips off the floor as high as possible, count to 10, and then slowly lower them to the ground. Repeat this movement 5 times.

 Superman

Tell the children: Lie on your stomach. Reach both arms overhead (as if you're Superman flying) and lift both arms off the floor. Pause and count to 5. Then lower your arms slowly.

 Bottom Walking

Tell the children: Sit on the floor. Lift your right hip, moving it forward, and then do the same with your left hip so that you can "walk" forward. Walk forward 10 times and backward 10 times.

 Sit Down, Please!

Props   A chair for each pair

Select a chair that is of the right height for a preschooler. Use a foot stool if it is a better height. Divide the group into pairs or have the players choose partners.

   Tell the children: Pick one partner to go first. Partner 1 stands in front of the chair, facing his partner and when they are both ready to start, partner 1 begins to sit down slowly. When partner 1 is halfway to sitting, partner 2 will say, "Stop!" at which time partner 1 needs to hold this position and count out loud for as long as he is able to hold it.

Tip   Play this game a few times and then have partners switch roles. It's a good game for parents, too.

45 I Grew!

Divide the group into pairs or have the players choose partners.

Tell the children: Pick one partner to go first. Partner 1, hold onto your partner's hands for balance. Then rise up onto your toes as high as possible. Count to 10 backward and then slowly lower yourself back down. Repeat this movement 10 times, and then switch roles.

46 Plank Position

Tell the children: Get on your knees and lean on your forearms on the floor. Straighten your legs behind you and use your back and stomach muscles to lift your stomach off the floor. Your body should form a straight line from shoulders to heels. Hold this position for a count of 3.

Variation When preschoolers are strong enough to hold their bodies in a straight line for more than 3 seconds, challenge them to try the plank position with straight arms and with fingers pointing forward.

47 Monkey Jacks

Tell the children: Begin this movement in a standing position, arms at your sides. Begin jumping up and down while alternately raising one arm and lowering the other. Repeat this movement for 30 seconds.

48 Lucky Leprechaun

Tell the children: In a standing position, jump up and click the heels of your feet together, beneath your body.

Bucking Bronco

Tell the children: Begin on your hands and knees. Now, kick up toward the ceiling with one leg at a time—first left, then right. Repeat this alternating movement for 1 minute.

Variation When your preschoolers are confident with this exercise, challenge them by asking them to kick up both feet at the same time.

Crab Walk

This exercise is good for all kids—and adults, too.

    Tell the children: Sit on floor with your knees bent and your feet flat on floor. Your hands should be behind your body with your palms flat against the floor and your fingers pointing away from your body. Lift your hips off the floor and walk backward using your hands and feet. Next, walk forward. Repeat this movement for 3 minutes.

Variation Turn this exercise into a race. Or put a toy on each player's tummy to see if the children can balance a toy while performing the Crab Walk.

Crab Kick

Tell the children: Start in the Crab Walk (#50) position. Keep your knees at right angles and keep your bottom off of the floor. Kick up your right leg. Then kick up your left leg. How many kicks can you do?

Duck Walk

Tell the children: Start with feet slightly apart. Bend your knees and lower your upper body toward your ankles. You should be in a low squat position. Grab hold of your ankles with your hands. Now walk forward 10 steps and backward 10 steps.

Rooster Strut

Tell the children: Start in a standing position. Place your hands on your hips with elbows out to the side. Alternate bringing each knee up before stepping forward. Extend your chin forward and back as you strut. Repeat this exercise for 1 minute.

Frog Jump

Tell the children: Start by placing both hands on the ground in front of your feet. Bend your knees. Reach forward with both hands, place them on the ground, and then jump both feet up toward your hands. Continue this movement, saying "rrrrrriiibiiiiit!" as you go. Repeat this movement for 3 minutes.

Star Tuck

Tell the children: Start in a star position by standing on the ground with your legs wide in a straddle position and your arms held wide overhead. Immediately come in to a tucked or a ball position, crouching down and wrapping your arms around your knees. Jump back up into a star position. Repeat this exercise for 1 minute.

Sit 'n Roll

Tell the children: Sit in a cross-legged position. Roll completely over to your right side, using your arms to assist and support your body, and then roll into a seated position again. Try this 5 times on your right side and 5 times on your left side.

Jumping Kangaroo

Tell the children: Stand with your feet together and your back straight. Bend your knees. Bend both arms at the elbow in front of your body, with your hands hanging in front of them. Jump with both feet at the same time. Jump forward, backward, left, and right.

Crocodile Crawl

Tell the children: Lie facedown on the mat. Place your hands on the floor in front of your body. Using only your arms, push your upper body up until your arms are straight. Your legs will remain on the ground. Keeping your elbows straight, begin to creep forward with your hands, dragging your feet behind you. Travel this movement around the room for 1 minute.

Slithering Lizard

Tell the children: Lie on the floor on your belly. Bend your elbows to a 90-degree angle. Move your left arm forward at the same time as you slide your left foot up toward your left hand, lifting your body off the floor, bring your left knee forward toward your left elbow, immediately repeat the movement on your right side, travel this movement for 1 minute.

Inchworm

Tell the children: Stand with your feet on the floor, shoulder-width apart. Next, bend over and place your hands flat on the ground in front of your feet. In this starting position, your bottom should be high in the air, and your body should look like an upside-down *V*. Walk your hands out as far forward as possible; your tummy should be almost on the floor. Walk your hands back to the starting position. Repeat this movement 10 times.

Building Strong Arms

Teach these movements individually; when the children show confidence in a movement, add a lower-body exercise with the arm movement to teach balance and coordination. Lower body movements that work well with these exercises are running, walking, jumping, leaping, shuffling, walking backward, squat jump, skipping, and hopping on one leg.

61 Breaststroke Arms

Tell the children: Extend both arms to the front, palms turned down. Raise your arms over your head, and then move them to the side to form a Y shape with your body. With your arms straight and back behind your body, bend your elbows and bring your arms close to your body. Push your arms forward and extend them into the starting position again. Repeat this movement 10 times.

62 Crawl Arms

Tell the children: This is just like the swimming stroke. Bend your right arm and in a circular motion, extend your arm out in front of your body. Then bend your left arm and circle it in front of your body. Repeat this exercise for 30 seconds.

Tip To make this movement fun, the leader should instruct the children to start slow and then speed up.

63 Backstroke Arms

Tell the children: Rotate your arms in a backward circle, alternating them. Make sure you make big circles. Repeat this movement 10 times.

Doggie-Paddle Arms

This movement copies the movement of a swimming dog.

Tell the children: Extend your right arm in front of you, palm down. Bring your left arm in front of your chest, palm down. Scoop the right arm down and back in front of your body while your left arm extends in front of you. Now scoop the left arm down and back in front of your body while your right arm extends in front of you. Repeat this exercise 10 times.

 ## Windshield-Wiper Arms

Tell the children: Bring both of your arms up in front of your body, and bend your arms upward at the elbows. Now sweep your arms together from one side to the other. Repeat this exercise 10 times.

 ## Paddleboat Arms

Tell the children: Bring your arms out in front of your body, with your palms down, and bend your arms inward at the elbows. Make a fist with each hand. Place one fist above the other fist so that they are about 4 inches apart and begin to rotate the hands in a circle. Repeat this movement 10 times.

Variation To challenge the children's coordination, have them reverse the circle.

 ## Punching Arms

Tell the children: Make fists with both hands. Bring one hand up in front of your chin, like a boxer, to protect your face while the other hand punches forward. Repeat this movement 10 times.

Variation To challenge the children's coordination, have them reverse the positions of their hands.

Chicken Arms

Tell the children: Place your thumbs in your armpits. Flap your elbows up and down like a chicken. Repeat this movement for 30 seconds.

Bow-'n-Arrow Arms

Tell the children: Extend both arms in front of your body at shoulder height. Make a fist with each hand, holding your thumbs upward. Keeping your left arm extended, bend your right elbow and slide that elbow back toward your right shoulder, as if you are pulling back the string on a bow. Return your arm to the starting position. Repeat this movement 10 times.

Variation When the children feel confident with this movement, have them switch arms.

Baseball Swing

Tell the children: Imagine holding a baseball bat and swinging it through the hit. Now imagine switching the position of the bat, as if you're going to bat from the opposite side. Be sure to swing your arms through. Repeat this movement for 30 seconds.

Overhead Pass

pairs

Divide the group into pairs or have the players choose partners.

Tell the children: Pick one partner to go first. Partner 1, with both arms overhead, imagine holding onto a basketball. Throw the ball to partner 2. Now it's the other partner's turn to pass the ball. Repeat this exercise for 1 minute.

Yippee Arms

Tell the children: Raise both of your arms up over your head. Circle your arms in a very big circle and yell, "Yippee!" Now try it again, circling your arms the opposite way. Repeat this movement 10 times.

Chest-Pass Arms

pairs

Divide the group into pairs or have the players choose partners.

Tell the children: Pick one partner to go first. Partner 1, imagine passing a basketball to your partner. Bring both arms up to chest height, bending elbows and forcefully extending arms straight out in front of your body. It is now the other partner's turn. Each player should repeat the movement 10 times.

Bowling Arms

Tell the children: This movement copies the move of rolling a bowling ball. Start this movement by bringing both hands toward your chest. In one motion, step forward with the left foot. Swinging your right hand behind your body, step forward with your right foot and then swing your right arm forward, as if tossing the ball. To repeat the movement from the beginning, bend your right arm back into the chest and repeat with the left arm. Repeat this movement 10 times with each arm.

Golf-Swing Arms

Tell the children: Stand with your legs slightly apart. Lower your arms, bringing your hands together. Bending slightly at the waist, pull your arms back to one side and then swing through as if you are playing golf. Repeat this movement 10 times.

76   Tennis Arms

Tell the children: Using your imagination, play a game of tennis. Swing your arm in front of your body from low to high positions, pretending you are hitting a tennis ball with a racket. Now swing your arm from high to low positions. Repeat this movement 10 times.

Strengthening the Heart Muscle

Aerobic exercises are activities that challenge the heart to beat faster and increase the depth and rate of breathing. Getting aerobic exercise on a regular basis can strengthen the heart and lungs.

These exercises are combination patterns that will elevate the heart rate. In addition, they will challenge children's coordination sills. Try each exercise separately. Then, when the children show confidence in a movement, combine multiple patterns together.

 ## 77   Walk and Jump

Tell the children: Walk forward 8 steps; jump up 8 times. Turn around and walk back to the starting point. Repeat this combination 10 times.

Forward and Backward

Tell the children: Run forward for 20 steps. Then take 10 big steps backward. Repeat this sequence 5 times.

 ## Toe-Tapping

Tell the children: Walk forward 4 big steps. Toe tap out to each side 8 times. Then take 4 big steps backward and toe tap out to each side 8 times. Repeat this combination 4 times.

 ## Shimmy Shoulders

Tell the children: Walk in a circle, and then walk in a circle while shaking your shoulders. Do this combination 4 times and then do the same combination 4 times going backward.

 ## Karate Kids

Tell the children: Start in a standing position. Lift your left leg and kick out to the left side 5 times. Bring your left leg back into a standing position and kick out your right leg to the right side 5 times. Bring your right leg back into the starting position and punch forward 10 times, alternating arms. Repeat the entire sequence 5 times.

 ## Hop and Roll

Tell the children: Bunny Hop (#196) forward 8 times and then Tootsie Roll (#178) back to the starting position. Repeat this sequence 5 times.

Shuffling Jacks

Tell the children: To do a shuffle step, start with your feet together and, without lifting one of your feet off the floor, slide it to the side and then slide your other foot along the floor to meet it. Shuffle to your right 4 times. Stop. Do 4 Jumping Jacks (#173). Shuffle back to the center and do 4 more Jumping Jacks. Shuffle to your left 4 times, do 4 Jumping Jacks, and then shuffle back to the center and do 4 more Jumping Jacks. Repeat this sequence 5 times.

 # Pop and Slide

Tell the children: Popcorn Game jump (#2) 8 times. Then Step Slide (#299) 4 times to one side and then 4 times to the opposite side. Repeat this sequence 5 times.

 # Kick and Hop

Tell the children: Do 10 High Kicks (#182) moving forward. Stop and then do 20 Bunny Hops (#196) backward to where you started. Repeat this combination 10 times.

 # Soar Like an Airplane

Tell the children: Begin running in a big circle with your arms extended at shoulder height as if they are airplane wings and count out loud to 20 while doing Airplane (#138) arms. Stop and repeat, running in a circle in the opposite direction. Repeat this 4 times and then do 10 Tuck Jumps (#181). Repeat this entire sequence 5 times.

87 Frog Legs

Tell the children: Frog Jump (#54) 10 times. Then do Tiptoes (#190) back to the starting position. Repeat this combination 5 times.

88 Dizzy Dance

Tell the children: Starting from a standing position, twirl around in a circle 2 times. Rooster Strut (#53) forward 10 steps and then Bear Crawl (#35) back to the starting position 10 steps. Repeat this entire sequence 3 times.

89 Shake It Off

Tell the children: Shake your feet as if you have something stuck on the bottom of your shoe! Shake your left foot 10 times, counting out loud, then shake your right foot 10 times, and then shimmy your shoulders while counting to 10. Repeat this sequence 5 times.

90 Leap and Crawl

Prop A soft surface

Divide the group into pairs or have the players choose partners.

Tell the children: Player #1, kneel on the ground, rest your head on the ground, and cover it with your hands. Player #2, place your hands on the back of Player #1 and then press on the person's back to help you leap over them while spreading your legs apart and hopping like a frog. Player #2, remain standing with your legs apart while Player #1 crawls through your legs. Repeat this 10 times and then switch roles. Repeat this combination 2 times so both partners can leap and crawl.

 **Flicker**

Tell the children: Flick Kick (#300) 20 times. Then, in a Triangle Gallop (#194), make 4 circles. Repeat this sequence 5 times.

 Ballet Legs

Tell the children: Rond (#303) 10 times on each foot. Gazelle (#197) 5 times in one direction and then leap 5 times in the other direction. Then Rond 10 times on each foot again. Repeat this sequence 4 times.

 Skip, Twirl, and Jump

Tell the children: Skip (#198) 50 times, twirl 5 times, and Popcorn Game (#2) jump 10 times. Repeat this sequence 1 more time.

 Make Me Laugh

Tell the children: Run Like Grandma (#151) 20 times, make Chicken Arms (#68) 20 times, and do Imaginary Bicycle (#37) 20 times. Repeat this sequence 1 more time.

 Step, Swing, and Hold

Tell the children: Fox Trot (#293) 4 times, Golf-Swing Arms (#75) 20 times, and do a Plank Position (#46) for a count of 5. Repeat this sequence 5 times.

---

96 **Kickin' Tootsies**

Prop A pillow (or any small item that a child can step on and straddle) for each participant

Tell the children: Do 10 High Kicks (#182) forward, do 10 Straddle Steps (#180), and Tootsie Roll (#178) 10 times. Repeat this sequence 1 more time.

 97 **Slide and Roll**

Prop A jump rope

Tell the children: Slide (#187) sideways 4 times, Step, Knee (#195) 10 times, Broad Jump (#170) 10 times, and Sit 'n Roll (#56) 5 times. Repeat this sequence 5 times.

 98 **Tuck and Jump**

Tell the children: Star Tuck (#55) 10 times, Skip (#198) 10 times, and Frog Jump (#54) 10 times. Repeat this sequence 2 times.

 99 **Challenge Your Balance**

Tell the children: In a standing position, spin around in a circle 4 times, immediately stand on your right leg for 15 seconds. Spin around in the other direction 1 more time and stand on your left leg for 15 seconds. Repeat this sequence only once.

On the Farm

Tell the children: Do Chicken Arms (#68) 20 times, Rooster Strut (#53) 20 times, and Step on That Bug (#38) 20 times. Repeat this sequence 2 times.

 ## Broadway Show

Allow the music to help the children dance their way through this routine. Begin the music and have fun with this combination.

    Tell the children: Knee Pop (#291) 10 times, do 10 High Kicks (#182) going backward, and Gazelle (#197) forward 10 times. Repeat this sequence 3 times.

 ## Getting-Fit Combination

Props A jump rope; a door handle or another person

Tell the children: Do Jumping Rope 101 (#175) 20 times, do 4 Forward Rolls/ Somersaults (#183), and do 10 Bear Crawls (#35). Repeat this sequence 3 times.

 ## Down Under

Tell the children: Do Jumping Kangaroo (#57) 10 times, Star Tuck (#55) 10 times, and Side Lunge (#184) 10 times. Repeat this sequence 3 times.

Swimming Combination

Tell the children: Breaststroke Arms (#61) with walking 20 steps, Popcorn Game jump (#2) 10 times, and Star Tuck (#55) 10 times. Repeat this sequence 3 times.

 ## Worms

Tell the children: Inchworm (#60) 10 times, Star Tuck (#55) 10 times, and Baseball Swing (#70) 20 times. Repeat this sequence 3 times.

 ## Reptile Challenge

Tell the children: Slithering Lizard (#59) 10 times, Crocodile Crawl (#58) 10 times, and Windshield-Wiper Arms (#65) 20 times. Repeat this sequence 3 times.

 ## Coordination Challenge

Tell the children: Scarf It Up (#243) 10 times, Step Slide (#299) 10 times, and do Windshield-Wiper Arms (#65) 20 times. Repeat this sequence 3 times.

 ## Get Down

Tell the children: Duck Walk (#52) forward 10 times; Step on That Bug (#38) 10 times, and Bear Crawl (#35) backward 10 times. Repeat this sequence 3 times.

Core Challenge

Tell the children: Do 10 Jumping Jills (#174), V Sit (#141) hold for 10 seconds, and Sit 'n Roll (#56) 10 times. Repeat this sequence 3 times.

 ## Cardio Combination

Tell the children: Do 10 Tuck Jumps (#181), Skip (#198) 10 times, and do Tennis Arms (#76) 20 times. Repeat this sequence 3 times.

 ## Let's Dance

Tell the children: Gancho (#298) 4 times, do 20 High Kicks (#182), and do Chicken Arms (#68) 10 times. Repeat this sequence 3 times.

 ## Leg Challenge

Tell the children: Lucky Leprechaun (#48) 4 times, Jumping Kangaroo (#57) 10 times forward, Rond (#303) 4 times each leg, and Frog Jump (#54) backward 10 times. Repeat this sequence 3 times.

 ## Yoga-Class Combination

Tell the children: Sit 'n Roll (#56) 4 times, V Sit (#141) 4 times, and Plank Position (#46) for as long as you can. Repeat this sequence 3 times.

Strut, Tuck, and Roll

Tell the children: Rooster Strut (#53) 10 times sideways, Star Tuck (#55) 10 times, and Tootsie Roll (#178) 10 times. Repeat this sequence 3 times.

 ## Tricky Legs

Props A pillow or any small item that a child can step on and straddle for each participant; a jump rope; a door handle or another person

Tell the children: Do 10 Straddle Steps (#180), Skip (#198) 25 times, and do Jumping Rope (#175) 25 times. Repeat this sequence 3 times.

 ## A Sweaty Head

Tell the children: Step Slide (#299) 10 times, Triangle Gallop (#194) 10 times, and Gazelle (#197) 10 times. Repeat this sequence 5 times.

 ## Animal Legs

Tell the children: Frog Jump (#54) sideways 10 times, Duck Walk (#52) backward 10 times, and Rooster Strut (#53) forward 10 times. Repeat this sequence 5 times.

 ## Funny-Looking Combination

Tell the children: Run in place 25 times with Yippee Arms (#72), do 10 Monkey Jacks (#47), and walk backward doing Backstroke Arms (#63) 10 times. Repeat this sequence 3 times.

Lucky Lizards

Tell the children: Slithering Lizard (#59) 10 times, Lucky Leprechaun (#48) 10 times, and Crab Walk (#50) 10 times. Repeat this sequence 3 times.

 Toe, Toe, Tootsies

Tell the children: Tootsie Roll (#178) 10 times, do 10 Tuck Jumps (#181), and Crab Kick (#51) 10 times. Repeat this sequence 3 times.

 Skip, Straddle, Kick

Props One pillow or any small item that a child can step on and straddle for each participant

Tell the children: Skip (#198) 30 times, do 30 Straddle Steps (#180), and do 10 Bucking Broncos (#49). Repeat this sequence 3 times.

 Go Backward

Tell the children: Run backward 10 times, Side Step (#147) 10 times, and run forward 10 steps. Repeat this sequence 5 times.

 Water Friends

Tell the children: Duck Walk (#52) 10 times, Crocodile Crawl (#58) 10 times, and Frog Jump (#54) 10 times. Repeat this sequence 5 times.

124 ## Cardio Moves

Tell the children: Do 10 Tuck Jumps (#181), run in a circle 4 times, and do 30 High Kicks (#182). Repeat this sequence 5 times.

 125 ## What Am I?

Tell the children: Bear Crawl (#35) 10 times, Crocodile Crawl (#58) 10 times, and do Slithering Lizard (#59) 10 times. Repeat this sequence 5 times.

 126 ## Aerobic Challenge

Tell the children: Do 10 Tuck Jumps (#181), Step Slide (#299) 10 times, and Skip (#198) 30 times. Repeat this sequence 5 times.

Fine Motor Skills

Demonstrate an exercise first.
Then teach the children how to perform it.

Learning to tie a shoelace, holding a pencil, painting, putting together a puzzle—these are all important accomplishments for preschoolers. Each achievement shows success with fine motor skills. These fine motor skills help develop dexterity, muscle strength, hand–eye coordination, and sensory perception. Developing fine motor skills is the building block for developing the larger motor skills, such as shooting a basketball into a hoop.

127 Finger Puppets

Preschoolers may have a hard time trying this exercise with their fingers, but this is a simple game that can be played even in the car. Tell preschoolers that they will be able to use all of their fingers.

Tell the children: Show me the numbers 1 through 10 using your fingers. Now use your hands and fingers to show me the shape of a ball. A piece of paper? Scissors? Walking legs? A bunny? A bird? A pair of glasses?

Variation Be creative and see if your preschooler can give you some challenging shapes to make.

128 Play the Piano

Preschoolers don't need to play the piano to learn how to manipulate their fingers.

Tell the children: Place both of your hands on a hard surface. Moving only one finger at a time, push down and pull up. Go through every finger on both of your hands, from pinkies to thumbs. Repeat this exercise 5 times.

Variation Have the children reverse the order, starting with thumbs and moving out to pinky fingers.

 Cotton Tail

Props Cotton balls or marbles

This game teaches children to use their toes in a whole new way. You will need a bag full of cotton balls to scatter around the floor. You can also use marbles.

Tell the children: Try to pick up a cotton ball using only your toes.

Variation For a more advanced game, set a timer to see how many cotton balls the children can pick up in a certain amount of time. Or set up a bucket, so the kids can release the cotton balls into a container once they've picked them up.

 Picky Fingers

Props Clothespins; feathers; paper

This game teaches children to manipulate their fingers to use a clothespin to pick up objects. This may sound easy to you, but when you are three years old, it is challenging. You will need a variety of objects such as cotton balls, crumpled paper, flat paper, feathers, and any objects that you think the children can pick up with a clothespin. Be creative.

Tell the children: Using a clothespin, pick up as many of these objects as you can.

 Pick-Up Sticks

Props Straws or sticks

Drop a box of straws on a large table.

Tell the children: When I say "Go," pick up as many straws as you can. Once you pick up one straw, you must transfer it to the other hand to hold until all straws are picked up.

Variation For older children, you can turn this game into a "beat the clock" game, to see how many they can pick up in a designated amount of time. You can also scatter the straws around the room, so the children will have to run from one straw to the other.

 ## Hold the Ball, Please...

Props A soft, small ball or balloon for each player

This exercise is meant to challenge preschoolers once they have successfully accomplished the games listed above for fine motor skills.

Tell the children: Tuck the ball between your chin and your chest. Hold it there as long as you can. If this is too easy, walk around the room while holding the ball in place.

Variation Have the players hold the ball between different parts of their bodies. For example:

- between the palms of their hands
- between their legs
- in an armpit

 ## Finger Catching

pairs

Props A soft ball or cotton ball for each pair of children

This exercise is meant to challenge preschoolers, but only if they have successfully mastered the skills listed in the previous games. Divide the group into pairs or have the players choose partners.

Tell the children: Toss a soft ball or cotton ball back and forth to your partner. Catch the ball using only your fingers.

Tip This is definitely harder than it sounds!

The Basic Building Blocks of Fitness

Your preschooler has something in common with every top athlete around the world, and that is every sport requires everyone to start with the most basic building blocks of fitness and then progress to more challenging movements, from the most simple movements to the most complex movements. This means performing a balance movement from a static position and then progressing on to a more challenging version involving dynamic balance or moving balance—such as when a toddler learns to climb a set of stairs, taking one step at a time.

 Praise the effort not the result.

The following physical activities are presented starting with the lowest level of difficulty. Always begin each activity at level 1. Then, when *children* feel they have achieved this level with ease, confidence, and skill, move on to level 2 or start with the first level in another activity (i.e., go from level 1 balance to level 1 in running, level 1 in catching, and so on. Gather all equipment you may need for each activity before starting.

At the end of this section I have included information on additional playful fitness activities.

Teaching Balance

 Demonstrate an exercise first. Then teach the children how to perform it.

Developing balance and coordination is just as important as strengthening little muscles. Balance is needed for everything our preschoolers do throughout their day, from climbing stairs to carrying a backpack to playing games. Balance is steadily emerging as children grow, and it can improve with practice.

Here are a few tips I use to teach kids how to make balancing a little easier:

- Have them focus on an object in front of them that is at their eye level.

- Make sure they breathe naturally; encourage children not to hold their breath.

- If any of the children lose their balance and begin to hop around on one foot, it's okay. Explain to them that the body is just trying to figure out how to balance in this new position.

- Tell them to keep their arms at chest height, unless you feel they want an additional challenge, in which case they can raise their arms over their heads.

 134 # Level I: Beanie Head

Props A beanbag or soft toy for each participant

This exercise works well with all ages. Place a beanbag or other soft toy on each child's head.

Tell the children: Try to walk from one place to another without dropping the beanbag.

Variations

- To make it easier, have the children hold the beanbags in place.

- To make it harder, have the children walk under or around things.
- Place the beanbag on another body part, like the back of the hand, shoulder, or elbow.
- Use a different toy or more than one toy.

 # 135 Level 2: Stork

Tell the children: Stand up and then lift one foot and try to balance on one leg for 15 seconds. Then put your foot down and try to stand on the other leg for 15 seconds.

Variation See if you and the children can invent ways to make the exercise easier, such as holding your arms out to the sides or overhead.

 # 136 Level 3: Walk the Line

Props Tape or chalk

Place a piece of tape on the floor, draw a straight line with sidewalk chalk, or walk on a curb. If the children are walking along the straight line of a curb, you may want to hold their hands—or pair children to work with each other—until each of them feels confident walking.

Tell the children: Imagine this chalk line is a tightrope. See if you can walk it without losing your balance. Focusing on the end of the line will help you keep your balance and make walking a little easier.

Variation Have the children try walking a straight line toe to heel.

Level 4: Close Your Eyes

This level will challenge children one step further by having them close their eyes and work on their balance.

Tell the children: Stand as straight as you can with your arms at your sides. Close your eyes. Now lift one foot off of the floor and hold this position for 10 seconds. Lower that foot back to the floor. Now lift your other foot off the floor and hold it there for 10 seconds. Lower that foot back to the floor.

 ## Level 5: Airplane

In the past four positions, the body is in the upright position. Now we will challenge children's balance by placing the body in a different position. Begin with children in a standing position.

Tell the children: Raise your arms out to the side at shoulder level. Balancing on your right leg, swing your left leg behind your body. Now bend at the waist, imagining yourself an airplane. Hold this position for a count of 10, and then slowly come back to a standing position. Repeat this exercise balancing on the other leg.

 ## Level 6: Modified Tree

Yoga is great way to teach children to balance. This common yoga position begins with participants in a standing position.

Tell the children: Shift your weight onto your right foot. Raise your left knee and place the bottom of your left foot on your right leg, at the ankle, calf, or knee. Raise your hands out to your side for balance. Hold this position for counting of 10, and then return to your starting position. Repeat this exercise with the other leg.

140 Level 7: Heel Up

Prop A chair (optional)

Tell the children: Start in a standing position. Shift your weight to your right foot. You may need to hold on to something, like a chair or someone's hand. Bend your left knee until your left heel comes up behind you. Without using your hand, pull your foot as close toward your buttocks as you can. Remain in this position for a count of 10. Then release this leg and try the routine with the other leg.

Variation Challenge children who are comfortable in this position: Ask them to grab their ankle and pull the heel closer to their buttocks.

141 Level 8: V Sit

Tell the children: Begin by sitting with your knees up and your feet on the floor. Slowly straighten your right leg so that the foot lifts off the floor. You should be balancing on your tailbone.

Slowly straighten the left leg, too, so both feet are off the floor. As your feet come up, your body should look like the letter V. Use your arms either to grab your legs for support or to extend out to the side for balance. Hold this position for a count of 10, return to the starting position, and repeat the exercise 3 times.

142 Level 9: Pointer

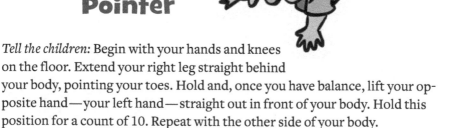

Tell the children: Begin with your hands and knees on the floor. Extend your right leg straight behind your body, pointing your toes. Hold and, once you have balance, lift your opposite hand—your left hand—straight out in front of your body. Hold this position for a count of 10. Repeat with the other side of your body.

143 Level 10: Side Plank

Tell the children: Begin this movement on your hands and knees. Put your arms straight below your shoulders and your fingers pointing forward. Now straighten your legs behind you to make the straight-arm Plank position, so that your whole body forms a straight line from head to toes. Keeping your right hand on the ground, turn your body to the left side, and hold this position as long as you can. Return to a plank position and switch to the other side.

By playing games to develop greater balance, children will recognize improvements in coordination, athletic skill, and posture. This, in turn, should result in fewer injuries and greater stability.

144 Freeze Tag

This game involves three or more players. This game is a lot of fun, but be sure to put a time limit on each game and give everyone the opportunity to be "the tagger."

Tell the children: This is a chasing game in which one person is "It." The object of the game is for the player who is "It"—the tagger—to tag as many players as she can within a time period. If a player is tagged, that person must freeze in the exact position he was in when tagged. But if an untagged player touches a frozen player, that player is thawed and can run freely again.

Variation To add a spin to this game, have the children suggest a theme for this game. For example, children may suggest that all the players must pretend they are animals or cartoon characters.

 **Statue**

This game requires 3 or more players.

Tell the children: One person is the director of the museum. The other players are the statues within the museum, and each player must think of a specific statue to be—for example, a statue of a dog, mouse, giant, dinosaur, bird. The director begins the game with her back to the statues, who have lined up against a far wall. When the director says, "Go," the statues run toward the director. If the director turns around, all statues must freeze. Any statue caught moving must sit out one turn. But if a statue makes it all the way to the director and tags her without getting caught, that player becomes the director, and the game begins again.

 Demonstrate an exercise first.
Then teach the children how to perform it.

Running is a great way to keep kids moving. It's easy to do and can be done almost anywhere.

 Level I: One Step at a Time

This particular level starts off all preschoolers with the confidence to accomplish this movement and to learn to count to 10 or higher! Begin by walking 10 steps; be sure to count them out loud. Then walk backward 10 steps, again counting out loud. Walk 10 steps to the right, to the left, and on a diagonal, each time counting out loud.

Tell the children: I will call out a direction—forward, backward, right, or left—and the number of steps to take. You will walk in the direction that I say—but don't forget to count your steps out loud as you walk.

Then, addressing players one at a time, you may lead them, calling out the direction and number of steps to take.

147 Level 2: Side Step

Walking and running sideways is needed for sports such as tennis and football. For a preschooler, this movement takes some coordination.

To begin, face the children so you can become their mirror and instruct them through this movement. Take a step to your side and bring the other foot along side to touch. Have the children do this with you. Repeat this exercise to the other side. If your preschoolers show confidence, take multiple steps to one side and multiple steps the other way. Or maybe you can mix it up, taking one step to the right and two steps to the left. At first, keep all movement lateral.

Tell the children: Face the front and watch my movements. Pretend you're looking in a mirror and see how closely you can copy the movements I make.

Variation Allow various children to decide how many steps to take, in what direction, and lead the group.

148 Level 3: Run with Me

This exercise is best done together with your preschoolers. Choose to run forward, backward, to your right, to your left, on a diagonal, in a circle, in a zigzag pattern. (Running backward can be difficult for some preschoolers, so start off walking backward first.)

Tell the children: Together, we will count out loud how many running steps we will take. I will call out the direction in which we'll run so we won't bump into each other.

Variations

- Let the children take turns calling out the directions for everyone to follow.
- Do this exercise with players in pairs. Assign each child a partner. Instruct the children to move in pairs, running forward, backward, in a circle, or even in a zigzag pattern.

149 Level 4: Adding On

Once you feel the children are ready to add on to running, add another variable. For example, have them run to a cone or a goal, jump up 3 times, run back to home base, and start again. Here are some fun add-ons:

- Monkey Jacks (#47)
- High Kicks (#182)
- Frog Jump (#54)
- Karate Kids (#81)
- Forward Rolls/Somersaults (#183)
- Walk and Jump (#77)
- Gazelle (#197)

Be as creative as you can.

Tell the children: Now that we know how to run together, I am going to tell you an activity to do in the middle of your running.

Tip This is a good opportunity to allow the children to come up with some silly movement for the end of your run. Be sure to copy them; that's what makes it so funny.

150 Level 5: *A* for Agile

Props Cones

This game includes listening skills. You will be the teacher first. Later you can switch roles with your preschoolers. To start, set up two cones about 20 feet apart.

Tell the children: On my command, run toward one of the goals. If I shout, "Stop and turn around!" you must stop immediately, turn around, and run in the opposite direction. Listen closely; I may ask you to do something other than run, such as walk, hop, or skip.

151 Level 6: Run Like Grandma

Sorry, grandmas, but the kids know exactly what I am talking about, and they think it's funny. This exercise adds variety to a run and challenges the children's legs. This exercise must be done together with the children.

Tell the children: Start off running as you would normally do and then bring your knees higher in front of your body. Next, run bringing your heels up toward your buttocks. The third funny movement is to run with your ankles kicking out to the side. The fourth movement is to pretend you are running on hot coals; your feet should barely touch the ground before they come back up into running position. It's okay to laugh; Grandma doesn't mind.

 ## Level 7: No Arms

This movement teaches children how to use their arms when running. First we take away all arm movement to help children understand how they use their arms when running.

To begin, have the children run toward you as you give instructions. You may want to perform the movements, too, so that everyone understands what to do with their arms.

Tell the children: Run with your arms at your sides; as best you can, keep them from moving. Next, run with your arms overhead; again, keep them from moving. Run with one arm up and one arm down. Run with your arms out to the sides of your body. Run with your arms making big circles; run and reverse the circles. Run with your arms punching in front of your body. Run with your arms swinging together at the same time. Run for 2 minutes.

Variation Let the children choose their desired way of swinging their arms as they run.

 ## Level 8: Interval Runs

This level incorporates speed and endurance in little amounts. Interval training for preschool level is not as serious as you may think. Invite your entire group (family, friends, preschoolers) to go for this run (and don't forget your dog, too.) Start out slowly and, after some practice, allow the children to call out the level of speed they prefer. Count each interval.

Tell the children: We'll start off walking. When everyone feels ready, we will increase our speed from slow to medium to fast. Later we can take turns calling out the speeds for the group.

Tip This exercise is designed for preschoolers to increase or decrease intensity of movement, not length of time.

Level 9: Take a Hike

Take your preschoolers to your neighborhood park. Running on a dirt path with hills is different from running on concrete. Be prepared with sunscreen and make sure the children have on the right clothing.

Tell the children: Start walking. If the path is safe—free of roots, rocks, and other obstacles—see if you can move more quickly. If you come to a hill, try running 10 steps up it.

Tip It is safer if you run up hills but walk down them.

Level 10: Go to the Beach or the Pool

Props A beach with sand or a shallow wading or swimming pool

Take your preschoolers to the beach or into the shallow end of the pool. Preschoolers will not be able to run for long periods of time because their muscles are working harder against the additional resistance provided by the sand or water. They will fatigue much faster than when running on hard surfaces. Don't forget to bring plenty of water and sunscreen.

Tell the children: Running on sand or in the water is much more difficult than running on land, but it is a lot of fun.

Relay Races

whole group

Props Cones

Relay races (see description on page 18) are a fun way to keep kids active. If you have 3 or more players, you can have a relay race. Here are some races that work well with preschool children. Set up a start and a finish line for the races, but remember that these games have no winners or losers.

Tell the children: I have set up a starting line and a finish line. Line up on the starting line, and on my word "Go," perform one of the movements listed below all the way to the finish line, when you reach the finish line, run back to the starting line and tag the next player on your team, who will now continue the race.

- running
- Duck Walk (#52)
- Bear Crawl (#35)
- Gazelle (#197)
- Frog Jump (#54)
- Crab Walk (#50)

 ## 157 Duck, Duck, Goose!

Tell the children: Everyone sits in a circle on the floor. One person is the "Goose," and the rest are the "Ducks." The goose walks around the outside of the circle, patting each duck on the head and saying, "Duck." Eventually, the player touches someone's head and says, "Goose!" The tagged duck then chases the goose around the circle. The goose tries to get back around to the empty seat and sit down before being tagged. If successful, the goose rejoins the seated ducks, and the new goose now starts the game again. If the first goose is tagged, she sits in the center of the circle as the game goes on. As more people get tagged, the circle gets tighter and the chase gets tighter! The last person standing is the goose.

 ## 158 I Wonder

Props One pedometer for each participant (purchase online or at any sporting-goods store)

Tell the children: Using a pedometer can be fun. A pedometer counts the number of steps you take. How many steps do you take per day? How many steps does it take to get from your room to the backyard? How many steps to walk to school? How many steps to your friend's house?

 ## 159 Red Light, Green Light

This is a great game for family and friends.

Tell the children: Choose one player to be "It." The other players move to one end of the playing field. When "It" calls out "Green light," the other players run as fast as they can to him. If "It" calls out "Red light," all players must freeze. Anyone caught moving must go back to the starting line. If one player makes it all the way to "It," she tags the caller and becomes the new "It," and the game starts over.

160 Sardine

This is a great game for families or a group of friends. This game is best played in a large area but it can be inside or outside. Since this game is played when it is somewhat dark, be sure your preschooler is not afraid of the dark. Turn off the lights in the house or play outside at night.

Tell the children: The person who is "It" hides. Everyone else counts to 50. When the players are done counting, they go and find "It." But when they find "It," they hide with him until the last person finds the group hiding.

161 Mother, May I?

Tell the children: Choose one person to be the mother. The other players are the children. All children line up at one end; Mother (a boy or a girl) is at the other end. The mother turns away from the children. The mother names the children in any order and gives each a direction, such as "Addison, you may take…5 steps forward." Addison responds, "Mother, may I?" to which the mother responds, "Yes, you may," and then the child moves forward 5 steps. If Addison forgets to say, "Mother may I?" he loses his turn. The first child to reach Mother wins and can take a turn being her. The mother can be creative with her responses; she can give baby steps, giant steps, bunny hops, steps backward…

162 Hide and Seek

Another fun game for friends and families.

Tell the children: Select one player to be "It." This player is the seeker, and the other players hide. "It" must cover her eyes and count to 50 while the other players run and hide. When she finishes counting, she must say, "Ready or not, here I come." The search for the other players begins. When the seeker finds a player, she will yell, "I see Kyle hiding in…" so Kyle knows that he has been spotted. This first person the seeker finds will then be "It" for the next game. The seeker continues searching until all players have been found.

163 Follow the Leader
whole group

This game can be used for any type of exercise or household chore and it's best for groups of three or more participants. An adult should lead this activity for the first round of movements, but after one round you can let a child lead the group.

Tell the children: One person is chosen to be the leader. Everyone else is a follower. The leader will lead the group through a series of movements, dances, and exercises. For ideas, you can use any movement in this book. Let your imagination guide you and your followers. Each round of play should last 1 minute.

164 Hot or Cold?
whole group

This is a great game to help teach preschoolers how to follow directions. It takes some reasoning and logic on their part. This game is best for groups of three or more participants.

Tell the children: Choose one player to leave the room. While this player is out, hide an object somewhere in the room. Invite the player to come back into the room to look for the hidden object. As the first player searches, the others give clues, saying, "Hot" when the player gets close to the hidden object and "Cold" if she moves away from it.

165 Time Your Run

Props A stopwatch or any watch with a second hand (many phones now have stopwatches, too)

Set a starting line and a finish line before beginning the game.

Tip Children may not be able to read a stopwatch, so you may need to read the time for them.

Tell the children: Time the speed of everyone in your family or group. Record the speed score; everyone will want to improve their time with each new run.

Variations A timed run can include many types of movement: speed walking, running backward, adding silly styles (see Run Like Grandma, #151) or alternating a run with a leap.

Jumping Exercises

Demonstrate an exercise first. Then teach the children how to perform it.

Jumping is a skill that is used in almost every sport. It requires timing and a sense of rhythm. So for these ten levels, I recommend the use of a jump rope to teach proper jumping.

166 Level 1: Let's Jump

Divide the group into pairs or have the players choose partners.

Tell the children: Hold hands standing side by side with your partner, and then begin jumping up and down. Do this for 30 seconds. Next, face your partner and hold both of his hands, and then jump up and down for 30 seconds. This exercise helps you to establish a sense of rhythm with a partner.

Variation While holding hands standing side by side, hop first on one foot for 30 seconds and then on the other foot for 30 seconds.

Tip Also, varying the speed (fast or slow) can increase the intensity of the workout.

167 Level 2: Jump-Overs

Prop A jump rope

Tell the children: Place a jump rope flat on the ground. Walk up to the rope and jump over it. After you complete 1 jump, walk around and step back in line so you can jump again. Repeat this exercise for 3 minutes or until each of you has completed this exercise at least 5 times.

168 Level 3: Snake

Prop A long jump rope (at least 9 feet in length)

The adult holds the jump rope at one end and moves it back and forth so the rope looks like a slithering snake. This exercise helps to establish eye–foot coordination.

    Tell the children: Line up. Each of you should take a turn at walking up and facing the jump rope and then jumping over the moving jump rope. The object of this game is to avoid stepping on the rope while it is moving by jumping over it.

169 Level 4: Jump-Ups

Props Soft objects

To prepare for this activity, find soft objects around your house that are 5 to 6 inches high. Set them up around a soft surface. Some objects I have used are stuffed animals, foam balls, pillows, and rolled-up towels.

    Children can take turns being the leader in each round. Play this game until everyone has had a turn being the leader.

    Tell the children: Let's play Follow the Leader. I will lead, and together we will jump over some objects and walk around others.

170 Level 5: Broad Jump

Prop A jump rope

For preschool-age children, this activity is best done indoors. That way, if they fall, they have something soft to land on.

Tell the children: Lay a jump rope down on the floor and stand with your toes at the edge of it. Use your arms to swing forward and jump as far forward as you can. Measure your distance and try again.

171 Level 6: 180-Degree Turn

Props Two stuffed animals (or other visual target) for each participant

To help children understand how to turn while jumping can be complicated. To make this activity easier, I use a visual target on each side. So get two soft objects—let's say favorite stuffed animals—and place a child between them, with one animal to the left side and the other animal to the right side. Make sure the stuffed animals are at least 3 feet away from the child.

Tell the children: Face one of the animals. Now jump up in the air and turn your body so that when you land, you are facing the other animal. Try it again but turn in the opposite direction so you don't get dizzy.

Variation Once the children feel confident with a 180-degree turn, encourage them to turn even more as they jump. For a 360-degree turn only one stuffed animal is needed. Place the toy about 3 feet in front of the child's body so they can use this as a visual target. Explain that they will jump up and turn in the air and land back down facing the stuffed animal.

172 Level 7: Catch and Throw

With children in this age group, it is best if an adult is one of the participants in each pair.

Props A soft ball for each pair

Have a child stand approximately 3 feet from you.

Tell the children: When I toss the ball into the air, jump up to catch it. If you drop the ball, we'll try again. But if you catch the ball, throw it back to me, jumping as you do. Repeat the exercise several times.

Level 8: Jumping Jacks

Performing a jumping jack might sound easy, but it takes time to develop the coordination and rhythm for this movement. To teach this movement, start with only the feet part of the movement. Repeat until the children feel confident in this part of the movement.

Tell the children: Stand with your feet together and your hands on your hips. Then jump your feet apart. Ready to add arms? Let's do the Jumping Jack at a really slow speed. Start with your feet together, arms down by your side. Now jump your feet apart, swing your arms up, and clap overhead.

Repeat each part of the movement as many times as necessary for the players to be successful.

Level 9: Jumping Jills

As with the Jumping Jack, start with only the feet part of the movement.

Tell the children: Stand with one foot in front of the other as if you are walking. Jump up and switch leg positions.

When the children have accomplished the leg movement, add the arm movement.

Tell the children: As you jump your feet apart, swing your arms in the opposite direction of your feet. In other words, if your left foot is forward, your right arm will also be in front and your left arm will be behind your body.

Level 10: Jumping Rope 101

Props A jump rope; a door handle or another person

To help children master a full swing jump rope, begin by tying one end of a jump rope to a stationary object, such as a door, or ask another person to hold the end. You hold the other end of the jump rope and swing the rope slowly back and forth. Depending on the height, age, and skill level of the preschooler, give the rope some slack and swing the rope very slowly until your preschooler is confident in jumping back and forth over the rope. Once the preschooler has mastered this level, you can make a full swing of the rope over their head.

Tell the children: Stand sideways to the rope and jump over it when it comes close to your leg.

176 The Wave

whole group

Prop A jump rope or rope at least 12 feet in length

This game is good for the entire family or group and works best in groups of 3 or more. The adult should twirl the rope. Children stand in a large circle. The adult or spinner stands in the middle of the circle twirling the rope on the ground with the opposite end of the jump rope passing under the children's feet. The rope should remain on the ground as it spins around the circle to avoid hitting the children in the shins. Repeat this game several times counting the number of successful jumps.

Tell the children: Stand in a circle about 6 feet away from the spinner. I will stand in the center and twirl the jump rope in a complete circle. Work together as a group to see how many times the entire group can successfully jump the rope as it makes a complete circle.

177 Hopscotch

small groups

Props A marker (rock, beanbag, etc.) for each participant

Hopscotch has many variations; this is one that preschool children can play. Use chalk to draw a hopscotch pattern. Create a diagram with 10 sections:

Tell the children: Each player has a marker. The first player stands behind the starting line to toss his marker into square 1. The marker must land inside the square. The player then hops over square 1 and through the rest of the course. Single squares must be hopped on one foot but when players come to a two-square section, both feet can touch down. At the top is a "safe" zone, in which a player can pause and turn around. Then he returns through the course until he reaches the square with the marker. Then he picks up the marker and continues the course without touching a line or stepping into a square with another player's marker. A player loses a turn if the marker is tossed into the wrong square or if he loses his balance. Players must then begin each turn where they last left off. The first player to complete one course for every numbered square wins the game.

Tumbling Exercises

Demonstrate an exercise first. Then teach the children how to perform it.

Tumbling exercises can improve a child's strength, flexibility, agility, balance, coordination, and self-confidence.

178 Level I: Tootsie Roll

Tell the children: Lie facedown on the floor with your arms extended over your head. Roll over sideways onto your back and continue the movement by rolling back onto your stomach. Continue the movement without stopping, rolling over and over again. Repeat this movement for 30 seconds.

179 Level 2: Full Squats
 pairs

Tell the children: Stand with your feet wider than your torso. Bend your knees, and lower your bottom until it's almost touching the floor, separate your thighs slightly, and lean your upper body forward so it fits snugly between your thighs. Press your elbows against your inner knees, bring your palms together, and hold the position for 15 seconds.

180   Level 3: Straddle Steps

Props   A pillow or any small item that a child can step on and straddle for each participant

Select a pillow that is large enough for children to step on but not too wide for them to straddle. Begin by demonstrating this exercise for the group. When the children can perform this exercise with ease, ask them to increase their speed.

   Tell the children: Step on to the pillow with both feet. Then move one foot off the pillow and straddle one side of the pillow; then move your other foot off the pillow to straddle the other side. The pillow should now be between your feet. Step back onto the pillow, one foot at a time. Repeat this movement 10 times.

181   Level 4: Tuck Jumps

Tell the children: Begin in a standing position. Bend your knees and jump up, bringing your knees up in front of your body. Slap your hands onto your knees and then return to a standing position. Repeat this movement 10 times.

182   Level 5: High Kicks

Tell the children: From a standing position, swing your right leg out in front of you as high as you can and then bring it back into a standing position. Immediately swing your left leg out in front of you as high as you can. Now circle the room using this movement.

183 Level 6: Forward Rolls/Somersaults

Tell the children: Begin in a crawl position. Tuck your head into your chest and push your bottom up and over until you roll over. If you need help, an adult or partner may help you by placing a hand on your head to keep your chin tucked under or by pushing your bottom over your shoulders.

184 Level 7: Side Lunges

Tell the children: Stand with your legs together. Take a big step out to your right side with your right leg, turning your foot 45 degrees to the outside and turning your body slightly on a diagonal so that your bent knees and your toes are pointing in the same direction. Keeping your back straight, bend your right knee and keep your left leg straight. Return to the center and repeat this movement on your left side. Repeat this movement 10 times on each side.

185 Level 8: Hula-Hoop Twirls

Props A hula hoop for each participant

Using a hula hoop teaches rhythm, timing, coordination, and momentum. Begin by demonstrating the movement on your arm first, and then let the children try.

Tell the children: Slide your arm inside the hula hoop and begin to move your arm in a circle. Once you are able to keep the hoop turning on your arm for more than 30 seconds, move the hoop to your other arm. Once you have mastered this exercise, put the hoop around your waist and spin the hoop using your hips. Repeat this movement 4 times with each arm.

186 Level 9: Camel Walk

Tell the children: Place your hands and feet on the floor. Keeping your back straight, walk by moving your right hand and left foot, and then your left hand and right foot. Repeat this movement for 30 seconds.

Variation To challenge the children's coordination, have them walk moving the right arm with the right leg and the left arm with the left leg.

187 Level 10: Sliding

Props A pair of socks for each participant; a slippery floor

This exercise teaches balance. Sliding also strengthens the inner and outer thighs. Begin by demonstrating how to slide on the floor. I do not recommend running and sliding until the children feel competent with all of the components.

Tell the children: Begin with an easy side-to-side slide. Next, turn sideways and perform a cross-country-skiing–style movement. Third, slide both feet apart at the same time but don't go too far. Slide your feet back together and begin again.

188 Limbo

Props Two people (or one person and a tree or other vertical post); a rope or pole

Music Caribbean music

The Limbo is a popular dance contest that originated on the island of Trinidad, so to keep this dance fun, play some Caribbean music. Tie one end of the rope to a tree or chair and hold the free side about 2 feet off the ground. (For this age group, it doesn't matter if the rope stays straight and taught or is slightly crooked and loose.)

Tip this game is best played on the grass or indoors on a carpet or over a mat.

Tell the children: Form a line with the first participant facing the rope. One at a time, go under the rope without letting it touch you, by crawling or scooting on your tummies. I will lower the rope a few inches after each successful pass. Make as many passes as you can and keep going no matter whether you touch the rope or not.

Variation "Animal Limbo": Have the children pretend they are a snake or other type of animal as they limbo.

Hopping, Skipping, and Leaping Exercises

Demonstrate an exercise first. Then teach the children how to perform it.

The following activities are heart-pumping, leg-strengthening exercises.

 189 ## Level I: Guess Who I Am Game

 whole group

Tell the children: Take turns imitating how a person, animal, or thing might move. The other players will guess who or what you are. Some ideas for people are tightrope walker, astronaut on the moon, window washer on a high ledge, old person, baby learning to walk, circus clown, or marching soldier. Animal suggestions might include penguin, kangaroo, bunny, horse, or snake. Add a change of direction to the game by doing your imitation walking backward, sideways, or on a diagonal.

190   Level 2: Tiptoes

Tell the children: Run on your tiptoes. Start slowly and go faster a little at a time. Run forward, backward, and in a zigzag pattern, making sure to stay on your tiptoes throughout each movement.

191   Level 3: Right or Left Leg?

Have children hop on their right foot then their left foot.

Tell the children: Hop on one foot. Begin with low hops and then slowly change your hop to a higher jump.

Talk with the group about which foot feels easier to hop on.

192   Level 4: Leaping with Streamers

Props Streamers

You will need long ribbons or streamers for this exercise. Begin by showing the children how to leap and have them leap across the room. Add variety to the leap by alternating the lead leg and then adding streamers.

Tell the children: Leap from one end of a room to the other. First leap leading with only your right leg; then leap leading only with your left leg. Now take streamers in one or both hands. Leap across the room again, this time carrying the streamers.

Level 5: Stair Climbing

Props Steps

Most children begin walking up stairs by taking one step at a time and leading with the same leg. Allow the children to do this until they are comfortable alternating feet as they go up stairs.

Tell the children: Most children learn to climb stairs taking one step at a time and leading with the same leg. Let's try that. When you are comfortable, let's use both feet to go up the stairs. Count or say the alphabet as you climb.

Level 6: Triangle Gallop

Tell the children: Stand with your back straight and tall. To gallop, step forward with one leg and slide the back leg up to the front leg. Once you feel comfortable doing the leg movement, reach your arms straight overhead and clasp your fingers together, allowing your arms to form a triangle with your body that will challenge your coordination. Travel this movement around the room for 1 minute.

Level 7: Step, Knee

The object of this exercise is to help prepare the children to skip. Practice this movement as many times as the children need to feel comfortable.

Tell the children: Start with legs together. Step forward with your right foot only. Your left knee bends up in front of your body and comes down immediately next to your right foot. Now step forward with your left foot. Bring your right knee up and then down, placing your right foot next to your left foot. Repeat this movement for 1 minute.

Level 8: Bunny Hop

Tell the children: Begin with your hands and feet on the floor. With both hands together, move them forward. Then with feet together, jump both feet forward. Repeat this movement several times.

197 # Level 9: Gazelle

The objective of this level is to leap from a stationary position and from moving positions.

Begin first by having the children practice their leaping skills. When leaping, children want to focus on distance and height.

Tell the children: Stand still and then leap forward. Repeat several times using the same leg to push off. From a standing position, alternate the lead leg as you leap. From a walking position, take 5 steps and then leap, again using the same lead leg. Switch the lead leg. Now from a running position, leap from the same lead leg. Then switch to the other leg. Repeat this exercise 10 times.

 198 # Level 10: Skipping

Practice skipping first and then demonstrate the movement to the children. Sometimes children have a hard time learning to skip.

To begin, be sure the children feel comfortable with Step, Knee (#195) on Level Seven. Practice Level Seven several times. Move on to running, add one knee lift, and run some more.

Tell the children: Now that you feel comfortable with Step, Knee, let's break down each movement of the skip: step forward right foot, knee lift left leg, and scoot. Say out loud "Step, knee lift, scoot forward," as you practice.

 199 # What Time Is It, Mister Fox?

whole group

The children gather on one side of the space, and the adult (as Mister Fox) stands on the other side.

Tell the children: At Mister Fox's signal, the players ask, "What time is it, Mister Fox?" Mister Fox answers, "It's time to hop!" Everyone hops toward Mister Fox until he signals you to stop. As you repeat this question, Mister Fox will substitute different movements (skipping, crawling, walking backward) until players draw near to Mister Fox. Then, as you again ask Mister Fox the question, the last answer he gives is "It's midnight!" At this point, he chases all the players back to the other side of the room. The game can then start again.

Sports-Performance Skills

Practicing sports is a fun way for kids to get outside, get some exercise, and also develop skills like teamwork and cooperation. Learning the fundamentals of a particular sport is essential to mastering youth sports. The following drills are exercises that teach players to develop basic skills in sports like soccer, baseball, and basketball.

Ball-Handling Skills

any size

Except as noted

Different types of balls teach different types of skills. For example, whiffle balls, basketballs, soccer balls, and sponge, rubber, yarn, bean, and fleece balls have various weights, sizes, surfaces, and designs that help develop grabbing, throwing, hitting, dribbling, bouncing, trapping, and other hand-eye coordination skills. Activities done outside and inside also teach children how different environments affect ball-handling skills, such as rolling a ball in the grass.

 Demonstrate an exercise first. Then teach the children how to perform it.

Rolling a Ball

Rolling a ball helps children to develop both hand–eye coordination and muscle control as they learn to control the direction of the ball as it leaves their hands.

 ## 200 Level 1: Trapped

pairs

Props A ball for each pair

Divide the group into pairs or have the players choose partners.

Tell the children: Sit opposite of your partner on the floor. Both of you should open up your legs into a V formation. Take turns rolling the ball to each other and trapping it with your legs. After you have trapped the ball, grab the ball with your hands and roll it back into your partner's legs. Repeat this exercise for 1 minute.

 ## 201 Level 2: Bowling 101

whole group

Prop A ball

Stand about 5 feet away from the children and roll a ball toward them. They will stop the ball with their hands and roll it back to you. As everyone becomes comfortable with this movement, increase and decrease the speed of the rolling ball.

Tell the children: When I roll the ball toward you, stop it and roll it back to me. As you get comfortable with this game, we can increase and decrease the speed and change the direction of the roll. Take turns so that everyone gets a chance to stop the ball and roll it back.

Variation If you have enough players, break into pairs to play the game.

Level 3: Roll and Stop

202

Props A ball for each participant

Begin by demonstrating this movement. This exercise is good for older children, too. Divide the group into pairs or have the players choose partners.

Tell the children: Roll a ball in front of your body slowly. Run to the spot where you think the ball will stop. Pick up the ball and repeat the exercise several times. The faster you roll the ball, the faster you will have to run to catch the ball.

Level 4: Bowling 102

203

small groups

Props A ball and several empty plastic bottles for each group

Place a large quantity of empty plastic bottles in a V formation, just like the set-up of pins in a bowling alley. You can vary the sizes and shapes of the bottles. Begin by demonstrating the movement for the children and then have them try. If they have a hard time knocking over the bottles, have the children stand closer to their target. As they start to feel competent with this game, have them move farther away again.

Tell the children: Stand about 10 feet away from the line of bottles. Roll the ball toward the bottles and try to knock over as many as you can. Set the bottles back up anvd try again. Repeat this exercise 10 times.

Level 5: OK, Roll!

204

pairs

Props Two balls for each pair

Divide the group into pairs or have the players choose partners.

Tell the children: Begin by rolling one ball at a time to each other. When you are ready, roll two balls at different times to each other, one right after another. To increase the challenge, roll the balls at different speeds and in different directions. Repeat this exercise for 3 minutes.

205 Level 6: Rolling for Agility

pairs

Props A ball for each pair

This exercise, which is best done outside, is a great partner exercise. Divide the group into pairs or have the players choose partners.

Tell the children: Start by rolling the ball to your partner's right side. As the ball is rolling, your partner runs toward it, stops it, picks it up, and rolls it to your right side. You must now run toward the ball and stop it. Repeat the exercise, rolling the ball side to side, forward, and backward. Repeat this exercise for 3 minutes.

206 Level 7: Mixed Bag

pairs

Props Several balls of different shapes and sizes for each pair

Divide the group into pairs or have the players choose partners.

Tell the children: With your partner, line up an assortment of balls. Take turns rolling the balls to each other. Be careful not to throw the balls; you must roll them. It's really fun if you can find an itsy bitsy little ball as well as a very large ball. Repeat this exercise for 3 minutes.

207 Level 8: Interval Speeds

whole group

Props Several soft balls

This exercise can be done with the children running from side to side or standing in a stationary position to catch balls.

Tell the children: The object of this game is to mix up the speed of the balls you toss to your partner or the group. Repeat this exercise for 3 minutes.

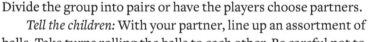

Level 9: Roll and Switch

Props A soft ball for each pair

This exercise teaches children hand–eye coordination. Divide the group into pairs or have the players choose partners.

Tell the children: Roll a ball to your partner with one hand. Your partner then repeats the same action. When the ball comes to you, catch it with one hand, switch the ball to your other hand, and roll it back to your partner. Repeat this exercise for 3 minutes.

Variation When the children feel competent with this exercise, have them repeat it using their nondominant hand to catch the ball.

Level 10: Rolling Obstacle Course

Props Balls, chairs; laundry baskets; tunnels; tubes; hula hoops, etc.

This exercise teaches the children to roll a ball through a target. Look around you for various targets and set up the targets around your fitness space. Demonstrate each course with the children. Smaller targets can be difficult for children at this age.

Tell the children: Roll the ball through or into the targets in this obstacle course. Repeat a target several times until you feel comfortable. Then move on to the next target.

Human Bowling Ball

Props Plastic bottles

This is fun for the entire family or group. This game should be played on a soft surface.

Tell the children: The object of the game is to knock over as many bottles as you can with your body. Set up the bottles. Either Crab Walk (#50) or Tootsie Roll (#178) your body into the plastic bottles.

Tossing/Throwing Skills

any size
Except as noted

Tossing or throwing games for kids are perfect to play outdoor or indoors. These games will improve hand–eye coordination in addition to simply being fun.

 Demonstrate an exercise first. Then teach the children how to perform it.

211 Level 1: Throwing 101

pairs

Props A big, soft ball or balloon for each pair

Stand close to the children as you teach them to throw a ball to you. Once they have mastered throwing and catching the ball, divide the group into pairs or have the players choose partners and have them toss the ball to one another.

Tell the children: Each time you make successful throw and catch, take a step back to make this game more challenging. If you drop the ball, both of you must step a step closer to one another and resume play. Repeat this game for 3 minutes.

At the end of this exercise, point out to the children the growing distance between partners, which is an indication of their success.

212 Level 2: Throwing 102

small groups

Props A soft ball and a target, such as a hula hoop, for each small group

Begin this exercise by demonstrating the technique. Throw the ball to a stationary object such as a hula hoop set up against a chair.

Tell the children: Throw the ball to a stationary object, such as a hula hoop set up against a chair. When you are able to throw the ball into the hoop 10 times, move the target farther away from you. Repeat this exercise for 3 minutes.

Variation Have players work in pairs. Have partners take turns picking up the hula hoop and slowly moving it up and down so that the child who is throwing the ball is working with a moving target.

213 Level 3: How Far?

Props A ball for each participant; stones or other small objects to mark a spot on the ground

This exercise is best done outside and with an adult watching where the ball lands so the spot can be marked. Don't forget to move the marker each time a child throws the ball.

Tell the children: Throw a ball as far as you possibly can. Mark the distance by placing a small object where the ball landed. Throw the ball again and try to beat the distance each time. Repeat this exercise for 3 minutes.

214 Level 4: Underhand Throw

pairs

Props A soft ball for each pair

It comes natural to most children to throw a ball overhand, so an underhand throw needs to be demonstrated and practiced. When children of this age first learn to throw underhand, they tend to toss the ball pretty high in the air. Divide the group into pairs or have the players choose partners.

Tell the children: The point of this exercise is to learn to throw underhand, keeping the ball low. Practice tossing the ball underhand just as I showed you. When you feel comfortable throwing the ball and keeping it low, work on throwing an underhand ball as far in front of you as you can. Repeat this exercise for 3 minutes.

Level 5: Overhead Throw

Props A big, soft ball for each participant

This exercise teaches the children to throw a ball overhead with both hands. Begin by demonstrating this exercise to the group.

Tip A basketball is too heavy to use in the beginning, so be sure to use a soft ball for safety.

Tell the children: Hold on to the ball and bring both hands over your head. Throw the ball toward a target using a horizontal movement. This exercise will teach you how to throw overhead for distance. Repeat this movement for 3 minutes.

Variation To have the children practice throwing the ball higher, have them toss the ball straight up into the air as high as they can and leave their arms overhead.

Level 6: Throwing a Baseball

Props A soft baseball; a target such as a hula hoop

Demonstrate how to throw a baseball, without the ball at first.

Tell the children: Hold the forearm of your throwing arm with your non-throwing hand to keep it stable, and practice throwing using just your fingers and wrist. Cock your wrist back at the top of the throwing motion. Place your index and middle finger across the top part of the ball. If you have smaller fingers, you may need to use three fingers instead of two to grip the ball. Tuck your thumb underneath and hold the ball out close to your fingertips. Point the lead shoulder of your nonthrowing arm at the target before throwing the ball. Then create a circular motion with the arm, bringing your hand down by your thigh and up around the shoulder, and throw the ball toward the target. Repeat this exercise for 5 minutes.

217 ## Level 7: Torso Twists

 Props A ball for each pair

Divide the group into pairs or have the players choose partners. Begin by having pairs toss a ball back and forth using two hands. Then to increase range of motion, demonstrate for the children how to rotate the torso by twisting one shoulder as far back as you comfortably can, and then releasing this coil while throwing the ball as far as you can.

> *Tell the children:* Stand opposite of your partner. Take turns tossing a ball to each other using two hands. Repeat this exercise, this time throwing the ball to each other from one side. Repeat, throwing the ball from the opposite side. Next throw a ball to each other from the side using only one hand. Repeat this exercise from the opposite side. Repeat this exercise for 3 minutes.

 218 ## Level 8: Granny Shot

Props A soft, large ball for each participant

I am not sure how this shot was named a granny shot, but my guess is that this is how most grandmothers toss up a ball. (I do not mean to offend any grannies.) First demonstrate this movement to the children.

> *Tell the children:* Holding onto a large ball, bend your knees and get into a squat position. Bring the ball down between your legs, swing your arms up, and release the ball. You will get some height from this shot, so it is best practiced outside. Repeat this exercise for 3 minutes.

 219 ## Level 9: Toss Everything

Props A variety of different objects (balloons, pillows, foam noodles used in pools, scarves, stuffed animals big and small, square items, tennis balls, etc.)

The objective of this exercise is to teach children to throw items other than balls. Gather several objects of various sizes, shapes, and weights and lay them on the ground in front of the group. Let the children feel what it is like to throw a balloon versus a ball. Discuss with them which style of throw feels best with each item.

Tell the children: Using only one item at a time, take turns throwing it toward a target. Be sure to try the different items. Which style of throw feels best with each item? For example, can I throw a scarf farther if I throw it overhead or underhand? Repeat this exercise for 3 minutes.

Tip Do not include any breakable objects in the lineup.

 220 Level 10: Frisbee 101

Props A small discus or Frisbee for each participant

Demonstrate throwing a Frisbee for the children.

Tell the children: When you are comfortable throwing a ball or other object, try throwing a Frisbee. This takes greater coordination. The release of the Frisbee comes from the action of your wrist. Repeat this exercise for 3 minutes.

 221 Marshmallow Basketball

Props A bag of marshmallows; paper bags; tape

This game is fun for all ages. If you're playing at home, be sure to include Grandma and Grandpa in the game.

Tell the children: Choose two players to be the hoops. Tape paper bags to their chests to make the hoops to toss the marshmallows into. Everybody else gets a handful of marshmallows. On "Go," everyone, including the hoops, moves around the play area. If you have marshmallows, try to toss them into the hoop players' bags. When all the marshmallows have been tossed, the game is over.

Tip The game is more fun if any participating adults are the marshmallow hoops first.

Variation Players can mark their marshmallows with a color marker to see who can make the most baskets or the hoops can compete to catch the most marshmallows.

222 Water-Balloon Toss

Props Water-filled balloons

This is a great game for a warm summer day. Divide the children into pairs. Give each pair one water-filled balloon.

Tell the children: Toss the water balloon to your partner from a short distance. Each time you are successful, take one step backward and do it again. If your balloon pops, get another balloon and start again from where you dropped the previous balloon.

Passing Exercises

Passing the ball through the air is a natural progression from rolling the bar to a partner, and takes even more muscle control, as it teaches children to control the direction and speed of the ball as it leaves their hands.

 Demonstrate an exercise first. Then teach the children how to perform it.

223 Level I: Thumbs Down

Props A ball for every pair

Divide the group into pairs or have the players choose partners. Try and get children to finish their passes by looking at where their thumbs finish, up or down.

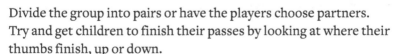

Tell the children: When you pass a ball like in basketball, as the hands release the ball, your fingers should spread apart and your thumbs should end up pointing down. Repeat this exercise for 1 minute.

224 Level 2: Travel and Pass

Props A soft ball for each pair

Divide the group into pairs or have the players choose partners.

Tell the children: Face your partner. Pass your object back and forth from this position. Once you feel comfortable doing this, walk side by side around the room while still passing your object. Repeat this exercise for 3 minutes.

Variation To make this movement more challenging, have the children pick up the pace to a jog.

225 Level 3: Passing the Baton

Props A baton or something in a cylindrical shape, like an empty roll of paper towels, for each pair

Divide the group into pairs or have the players choose partners. Once the children have mastered this movement, you can try a relay race.

Tell the children: Begin walking with your partner. One partner walks several steps ahead of the other. The partner in back walks up behind the lead partner and passes him the baton. The lead partner should extend his hand behind his body so his partner can place the baton into his hand without either partner stopping. Try passing the baton this way several times, and then switch roles.

226 Level 4: Supine Pass

Props A soft ball for each participant

Children begin by lying on their backs, face up. Each has a ball in her hands.

Tell the children: Lying on your back, pass the ball to your feet by lifting both legs up and toward your hands. Once the ball is between your feet, touch your feet to the floor and then bring them back up toward your hands. Pass the ball to your hands again. Repeat this exercise for 3 minutes.

227 Level 5: Stick Pass

Props A plastic golf club or hockey stick and a small ball for each participant

When you add a component to a movement—such as hitting a ball with a hockey stick—it may take preschooler some time to get the hang of it. Demonstrate the movement and then let the children try it.

Tell the children: Hold the hockey stick in both hands and place the ball in front of the stick. Gently push the ball with the stick. Once you feel comfortable with that, try hitting the ball. Repeat this exercise for 3 minutes.

Variation For an additional challenge, place a laundry basket on its side as a goal. Have the children try to hit a ball into the basket.

228 Level 6: Behind Your Back

Props A small, soft object for each pair

Divide the group into pairs or have the players choose partners. Partners begin this exercise by standing back to back. If a pair is made up of an adult and a child, the adult may have to kneel down.

Tell the children: Stand back to back with your partner. Pass your object from your hands to your partner's hands. Repeat this exercise for 3 minutes.

Variation If you have enough players, turn this exercise into a game. All players stand in a circle. Pass the object from person to person, with everyone keeping their hands behind their backs.

---

229 Level 7: Passing Around Your Legs

Props A small, soft ball for each participant

Demonstrate the movement first and then have the children try it.

Tell the children: Grab a ball in your hands and stand in a straddle position. Bend at the waist and, using one hand, pass the ball around the back of one leg and through to the front. There the other hand will grab the ball and pass it around the back of the opposite leg and toward the front, where the opposite hand grabs the ball again and continues the movement. Repeat this exercise for 3 minutes.

230 Level 8: Chest Pass

Props A large, soft ball for each pair

Demonstrate the movement first and then have the children try it. Divide the group into pairs or have the players choose partners.

Tell the children: Stand face-to-face with your partner and at least arms-distance apart. Bring the ball to your chest with both hands. Gently pass the ball from your chest toward your partner's chest. When he catches the ball with both hands, he will pass it back to you, chest high. Count how many times you and your partner successfully complete a chest pass. Repeat this exercise for 3 minutes.

231 Level 9: Soccer Pass

Props A medium-size ball for each pair

Demonstrate the movement first and then have the children try it. Divide the group into pairs or have the players choose partners.

Tell the children: Stand facing your partner, about 10 feet apart, and gently kick a ball toward her. Your partner will stop the ball and kick it back to you. Once both of you feel comfortable with this

exercise, stand shoulder to shoulder. Now pass the ball from your side to your partner and back, using only your feet. Repeat this exercise for 3 minutes.

Variation Try passing from side to side as you both walk forward slowly.

232 Level 10: Monkey in the Middle

small groups

Props A soft ball for throwing for each group of 3

Tell the children: Two players throw a ball back and forth, trying to keep it from the middle player. The ball may be rolled or tossed in any style—overhead, underhand, side throw, or overhand. If the player in the middle catches the ball, the player who last threw it and the middle player switch places, and the game continues.

Catching Skills

Kids love to throw and catch, whether it's a ball, pillow, balled-up sock, or Frisbee. Throwing and catching is good fun, good exercise, and excellent for developing all sorts of sport skills.

 Demonstrate an exercise first. Then teach the children how to perform it.

233 Level 1: Catching 101

pairs

Props A soft, large ball for each pair

In your own words, explain how to catch a ball to the children. Divide the group into pairs or have the players choose partners.

Tell the children: Sit down and play catch with your partner using a soft, large ball. Throw the ball back and forth. Practice catching the ball with both hands. Repeat this exercise for 3 minutes.

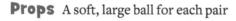

234 Level 2: Stand and Catch

pairs

Props A soft ball for each pair

Divide the group into pairs or have the players choose partners.

Tell the children: Face your partner and gently toss the ball toward him. When he catches the ball, he will throw it back to you. Keep throwing and catching. Count out loud how many times you are able to catch the ball. Repeat this exercise for 3 minutes.

235 Level 3: Catch Anything but a Cold

pairs

Props A group of objects—such as a towel, a balloon a pillow—for each pair

This game teaches children that objects will travel through the air at different speeds. It depends on the item being thrown. Divide the group into pairs or have the players choose partners.

Tell the children: Play catch in pairs. Toss any of your items to your partner one at a time. As your partner catches each, she will throw it back to you and repeat the game. Try to vary the height and speed of the items being thrown. Repeat this exercise for 3 minutes.

236 Level 4: Different Sizes

pairs

Props A variety of soft balls of different sizes for each pair

This exercise will teach your child hand–eye coordination, and speed and weight variations in catching a ball. Divide the group into pairs or have the players choose partners.

Tell the children: Your partner stands about 3 feet away from you. Toss different size balls to him. Watch your partner change hand positions when catching a small ball or a large ball. Repeat this exercise for 3 minutes.

237 # Level 5: Bucket Catch

 pairs

Props A bucket and ball for each pair

This exercise challenges children's hand–eye and hand–foot coordination. Instead of using their hands, preschooler partners learn how to catch a ball with another object. A bucket is a good tool to use when learning this skill. Begin by demonstrating the movement and then ask the children to try it. Divide the group into pairs or have the players choose partners.

Tell the children: On player throws the ball to the other, who catches the soft ball in a bucket. Take the ball out and play the game again. Be sure both partners get a chance to catch the ball with the bucket. Repeat this exercise for 3 minutes.

 238 # Level 6: S-M-F

Prop A ball

This game teaches children how to react when a ball is thrown at a slow, medium, or fast speed. Demonstrate this activity by teaching the children how to throw a slow ball. Then have them watch you catch the ball. Children will take turns working with you.

Tell the children: This game will help you react when a ball is thrown to you at a slow, medium, or fast speed. Practice throwing a slow ball, just as I showed you, and then practice catching one. Repeat this exercise for 3 minutes.

 239 # Level 7: Step and Catch

 pairs

Prop A soft, medium-size ball

Demonstrate this movement first. Divide the group into pairs or have the players choose partners.

Tell the children: Have your partner stand about four feet away, facing you. You can move out some if you both have good catching skills. Throw the ball so that your partner has to take a big step to the right or left to catch it. After doing this a number of times, switch roles with your partner. Repeat this exercise for 3 minutes.

Variation Have the catcher stand on one foot. One partner Throw the ball so that they have to take a few steps toward or away from their partner to catch the ball.

 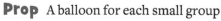

Level 8: No Catching

small groups

Prop A balloon for each small group

Tell the children: Throw a balloon up in the air. Try to keep it from touching the ground. Hit the balloon with different parts of your body, such as your nose, your elbow, your knee, and more. Repeat this exercise for 3 minutes.

Level 9: Hot Potato

whole group

Prop A small, soft ball

This game is extra fun when lots of friends or family members play along. One person needs to start and stop the music.

Tell the children: This game is fast, so pass and catch the ball quickly. Players stand in a circle or across from one another and turn on the music. Begin tossing the "potato" around to each player. When the music stops, the person who still has the "potato" sits down. The game continues until there is only one person standing.

Variation To avoid eliminating anyone, a person caught with the hot potato can only roll the ball to the other players.

 # Level 10: Crack Up

whole group

Prop A large, soft ball

Tell the children: One player is designated as "It" and has the ball. That player throws the ball at one of the other players. The player being thrown at can either dodge the ball or catch it. If the player is hit, he must count to 25 or sing the alphabet before he enters the game again. If the player catches the ball, he becomes "It," and the old "It" becomes a player.

Hand-Eye, Hand-Foot Coordination Skills

 any size Except as noted

Although the majority of the exercises within this book promote hand–eye or hand–foot skills, the following exercises focus on this coordination skill.

 Demonstrate an exercise first. Then teach the children how to perform it.

243 Level 1: Scarf It Up

Props A scarf for each participant

Divide the group into pairs or have the players choose partners.

Tell the children: Toss a scarf high in the air and catch it. Count how many times you can catch the scarf. Can your partner catch the scarf with one hand? Can she catch the scarf with her foot? Catch the scarf on your head. Throw the scarf and have your partner catch it. Repeat this exercise for 3 minutes.

244 Level 2: Hula-Hoop Rolling

Props A hula hoop for each participant

Demonstrate how to roll a hula hoop.

Tell the children: Place the hula hoop on its side. With your hand, firmly roll the hoop away from your body. See how long the hula hoop can roll. Repeat this exercise for 3 minutes.

245 ## Level 3: Soccer Stop

Props A ball for every pair

Divide the group into pairs or have the players choose partners.

Tell the children: Stand about 5 feet away from your partner and face him. Kick a ball to your partner and have him trap it with his feet. He will then kick the ball back to you, and you must trap the ball with your feet. Repeat this exercise for 3 minutes.

 246 ## Level 4: Drop Kick

Props A medium- to large-size ball for each pair

Divide the group into pairs or have the players choose partners. This exercise should be done outside where pairs will have enough room to really kick the ball. Demonstrate the movement for the group.

Tell the children: Have one partner take the ball in her hands, drop it, and kick it to her partner. The partner then takes a turn kicking the ball back. Repeat this exercise for 3 minutes.

Variation To challenge the children, decrease the size of the balls and try out different shapes of balls.

 247 ## Level 5: Knee Bump

Props A medium to large, soft ball for each participant

Demonstrate this movement first. This exercise is best performed outside.

Tell the children: From a standing position, drop your ball toward your knee. Bump the ball into the air with your knee. Repeat this exercise for 3 minutes.

Variation Eventually preschoolers may be able to bump the ball with a knee and catch it in the air.

Level 6: Balloon Tennis

Props Enough wooden paint stirrers, strong tape, and sturdy paper plates to make one racket for each player; balloons

Tape the wooden paint stirrers together. Then attach the stirrers to sturdy paper plates to make a rackets. Blow up some balloons.

   Tell the children: The object of the game is to keep the balloons from falling to the ground. Sit or stand but spread out across the floor and be ready with your rackets. Repeat this exercise for 3 minutes.

Variation See how long the children can keep the balloon aloft without it touching the ground.

Level 7: Two-Ball Toss

Props Two balls for each pair

This exercise requires hand–eye coordination and timing. Divide the group into pairs or have the players choose partners.

   Tell the children: Stand about 5 feet from your partner, with each of you holding on to a ball. On the word "Go," toss the balls to each other at the same time. Try to catch the ball. Repeat this exercise for 3 minutes.

Variation To challenge the children, have them step farther apart.

Level 8: Juggling 101

Props A ball for each participant

Demonstrate this movement first. Juggling requires top skills in hand–eye coordination and timing. For preschoolers, I begin to teach them the skill of juggling with only one ball.

   Tell the children: Hold the ball in one hand and toss the ball into the other hand. This may be as far as you can go at this point. That's ok; practice this movement as often as possible. The next step is to learn to toss the ball up and catch it with the opposite hand. Continue with this movement until you feel comfortable with it. The last step for this exercise is to toss the ball high, catch it with the opposite hand, and then toss it directly across to the opposite hand. Repeat this exercise for 3 minutes.

 ## Level 9: Teaser

Props A soft ball for each participant

Tell the children: Lie face up on floor with legs together, a soft ball balancing on your feet. Lift your legs and toss the ball up in the air. Bring your upper body up to catch the ball. Repeat this exercise for 3 minutes.

 ## Level 10: Shooting Balls
into a Basket

Props A basketball hoop or a large container to use as one; a ball

This activity will help with children's hand–eye coordination and depth perception.

Tell the children: Stand close to the basket or container to shoot baskets. As this becomes easier, move farther back. Shoot with two hands and then try shooting with one hand. As it gets easier, move the basket to different spots in the room. Repeat this exercise for 3 minutes.

Bouncing-Balls Skills

any size
Except as noted

Bouncing a ball is an important developmental skill for sports. It requires hand–eye coordination, rhythm, and timing. Plus, bouncing a ball is fun.

 Demonstrate an exercise first. Then teach the children how to perform it.

Level I: Basketball IOI

Props A kid's-size basketball or a vinyl ball for each participant

This activity will focus on children's timing and hand–eye coordination.

Tell the children: Bounce a ball while in a standing position. At first you may need to use two hands to bounce the ball. Repeat this exercise for 3 minutes.

Level 2: 2 to I

Props A kid's-size basketball for each participant

Tell the children: Bounce a ball with two hands. Then bounce the ball with one hand. Repeat this exercise for 3 minutes.

255 Level 3: Rhythm and Bounce

Props A kid's-size basketball or vinyl ball for each participant

Tell the children: Bounce a ball with both hands 3 times and then catch it. Repeat this activity for 1 minute.

256 Level 4: Sing and Bounce

Props A kid's-size basketball or vinyl ball for each participant

Tell the children: Bounce a ball with one hand for an entire song of "Row, Row, Row Your Boat" or "Twinkle, Twinkle, Little Star."

257 Level 5: Dribble

Props A kid's-size basketball or vinyl ball for every participant

This exercise adds movement to the basic dribble. It will challenge children's coordination skills.

Tell the children: Bounce a ball with one hand while taking a few steps. Do this several times. For more of a challenge, dribble forward, backward, and then side to side. Repeat this exercise for 3 minutes.

258 Level 6: Dribble Obstacle Course

Props Chairs; other obstacles; a basketball or vinyl ball

Set up the obstacles for the children to dribble the ball around. Leave plenty of room to go around each obstacle.

Tell the children: Start by dribbling. Continue dribbling in and around the obstacles.

259 **Level 7: Dribble Partner**

Props A basketball for each pair

Divide the group into pairs or have the players choose partners.

Tell the children: Bounce your ball toward your partner. Have your partner catch the ball and bounce it back. Repeat this exercise for 3 minutes.

Variation If the children want more of a challenge, have them step farther away from their partners.

 260 **Level 8: All Ball**

Props A variety of balls of all sizes

It is one thing to bounce and control a ball of one size. This exercise challenges children's skills by adding different sizes of balls.

Tell the children: Try bouncing tennis balls, ping pong balls, super bouncy balls, and big balls with one hand. Use the skills you learned in the last few activities to practice with the different-size balls. Repeat this exercise for 3 minutes.

 261 **Level 9: Four Square**

Props A medium-size rubber ball; chalk

This game is made simple for preschool children. You will need four players, a medium-size rubber ball, and chalk to draw a court with four large squares. Number each square from 1 to 4, so that 4 is opposite 1, and 3 is opposite 2. The object of this game is to move into the "king/queen" position in the box, which is square 4.

Tell the children: Each player takes a square. The ball must be bounced within the square of each player and can only be hit using hands. The king or queen, in square 4, begins the style of bounce (single bounce, double bounce, clap and bounce, turn around and bounce, etc.), then passes the ball to square 1. Square 1 must pass the ball to square 2, square 2 must pass the ball to square 3, and square 3 must pass the ball to square 4. If a player misses a square or does not perform the bounce correctly, he moves to square 1, and everyone advances.

 262 # Level 10: King of Stinky Socks

 whole group

Prop A ball of socks

You need a pair of socks rolled up in to a ball. The game is especially funny if the socks are stinky.

Tell the children: One player, called the king (a boy or girl), stands in the middle of a circle with all other players around him. The king throws the sock ball high into the air and calls out one person's name. That person must run into the circle and catch the sock ball before it hits the ground. If he does, that person is the new king. But if he misses, the player goes back in to the circle.

Tip If you are playing with young children, have the king toss the ball of socks to the preschooler.

Kicking Skills

any size
Except as noted

Kicking skills develop leg strength, locomotion, speed, and eye–foot coordination skills.

 Demonstrate an exercise first. Then teach the children how to perform it.

 ## Level 1: Kicking 101

Props A variety of different balls

The object of this activity is for children to get the feel of kicking a stationary ball.

Tell the children: Line up a variety of balls: a round ball, a football, a big ball, a small ball. Then take turns going down the line and kicking each one to get the feel of the different kinds. Repeat this exercise 20 times.

 ## Level 2: Kicking a Rolling Ball

pairs

Props A medium- to large-size ball for each pair

Divide the group into pairs or have the players choose partners.

Tell the children: Slowly roll a ball toward your partner and have her kick the ball. Try this several times and then switch roles. Repeat this exercise for 3 minutes.

265 Level 3: Set a Goal

Props A ball for each participant; two cones or objects to set up a goal

Set up two cones or other object allow two cones or enough space in between the cones for your goal.

Tell the children: Kick your ball in between the cones or objects. Repeat this exercise for 3 minutes.

266 Level 4: Laces Only

Divide the group into pairs or have the players choose partners.

Props A medium- to large-size soccer ball for each pair

Tell the children: Stand about 10 feet away from your partner. Place the ball on the ground and back up two steps. Step toward the ball, planting your non-kicking foot 3 to 5 inches from the side of the ball and kicking the soccer ball with the inside of your foot, about where the laces of your shoe go. Once the ball is kicked, your partner will trap the ball with his feet and repeat the kick back to you. Repeat this exercise for 5 minutes.

267 Level 5: Nondominant Foot

Props A medium- to large-size ball for each pair

Divide the group into pairs or have the players choose partners. Before starting this exercise, explain to the children what a nondominant foot is.

Tell the children: Stand 10 feet away from your partner. You will now kick the ball with your nondominant foot only. Practice kicking the ball to your partner. She will trap the ball and use her nondominant foot to kick the ball back to you. Repeat this exercise for 3 minutes.

Level 6: Get a Rhythm

Props A medium- to large-size ball for each pair

The children are ready to establish consistency and a sense of rhythm in kicking a ball. Divide the group into pairs or have the players choose partners.

Tell the children: Stand 8 feet away from your partner and kick a ball back and forth. Count how many times you can do this. When you and your partner can kick the ball to each other 10 times in a row, step farther away from each other and begin again. Don't allow too much time in between kicks. Once you receive the ball, kick it right back to your partner. Repeat this exercise for 3 minutes.

Level 7: No Swinging

Props A medium- to large-size ball or a football

Most children kick a ball with a big back swing of the leg. This exercise focuses only on the front part of the kick. It is not as easy as it sounds.

Tell the children: Place the ball just in front of you. Kick it by moving your leg forward, but don't backward to start the movement. Repeat this exercise for 3 minutes.

Variation Have the preschoolers try this exercise with the nondominant foot, too.

Level 8: Creative Teamwork

Props Four cones of different colors; one ball (the bigger, the better)

Place four cones of different colors in the four corners of your space.

Tell the children: Players gather in the middle of the space with the ball in the center. One player calls out the color of a cone, and then you must decide

---

as a team how to get the ball from the middle of the room to that cone. Everyone must participate, so you pass the ball in some form from one player to another. Some creative ideas to move the ball are rolling the ball from player to player, kicking it, carrying it, or moving it using the Crab Walk (#50) or Running Like Grandma (#151). When you reach the first cone, call out the color of another cone. The team then repeats the process. Do not use the same movement twice. Play this game for 10 minutes.

271 Kick the Can

Props A can

Tell the children: You will need friends, family, and a can. Put the can in an open space in the middle of your backyard. One person, selected to be "It," covers his eyes and slowly counts to 10 out loud while the other players run and hide. "It" then tries to find and tag each of the players. Any player who is tagged is sent to a "jail"—usually a spot around the can. Any player who is not caught can kick the can. This releases all players in jail, and the game continues. If "It" tags all the runners, a new game begins, and someone else is "It." The new "It" is usually the person who has been in hiding the longest or who has not been tagged.

Except as noted

Bat-, Racquet-, and Golf-Swinging Skills

Children must establish a comfort level with gross motor skills in order to move on to more challenging physical activities such as swinging a bat. Swinging exercises require crossing the midline of the body. To cross the midline, a child has to move her large upper-body muscles across her body and use both sides of her body simultaneously.

Demonstrate an exercise first. Then teach the children how to perform it.

272 Level I: No Bat Needed

Props A foam ball

Hitting a ball takes timing and hand–eye coordination. Because preschoolers haven't developed a good sense of timing yet it's a good idea to tell them when to swing.

Tell the children: I will stand about 5 feet in front of you. You should stand with your opposite shoulder pointing in my direction, just like in baseball. I will then toss the foam ball softly toward you at about your chest level and you will try to hit it.

Tip When you feel the child should swing, tell them. Repeat this exercise 10 times with a verbal cue, and then try pitching the ball without telling them to swing 10 times.

Level 2: No Ball Needed

Props A plastic or foam bat

This activity teaches children how to hold a bat properly and the technique for swinging it. Demonstrate how to hold a bat first; be sure to show the children how fingers grip the bat. I advise children to choke up on the bat so its mass is reduced and they can feel more control. Next demonstrate how to swing the bat. (Be sure to do this slowly.)

Tell the children: Begin this exercise by practicing how to hold the bat. Remember how your fingers should grip it. Next practice swinging the bat. How should you position the rest of your body when swinging? Repeat this exercise for 3 minutes.

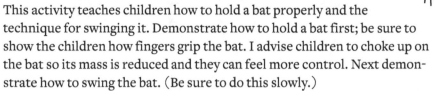 ## Level 3: Racquet Sports

Props An appropriately sized badminton, tennis, squash, or racquetball racquet; a small ball for each participant; a solid wall such as a ball wall or garage door

Before starting this exercise, demonstrate hitting a ball with a racquet.

Tell the children: In this exercise you will hit a ball off a wall, so it comes back to you and you can hit it again. See how many times you can hit the ball to the wall without letting it get away from you. Repeat this exercise for 5 minutes.

 ## Level 4: T-Ball

Props A T-ball stand; soft foam ball; plastic bat

Place a ball on a stationary stand like a T-ball stand.
Tell the children: Using a plastic bat, take turns swinging at the ball. Repeat this exercise for 5 minutes or longer.

276 Level 5: Sword Challenge

Props A plastic sword (or an item that is about the same size) for each participant

This exercise teaches children how to swing an instrument at different heights and with different motion.

Tell the children: Thinking about the Star Wars movies, practice swinging a sword overhead, up and down, and in big and little circles. Do not swing your sword at any of the other players. Repeat this activity for 3 minutes.

277 Level 6: Golf 101

Props A plastic golf club for each participant; foam balls

Tell the children: To practice another type of swing skill, take turns swinging a plastic golf club. Soft foam balls on the ground will make great targets. Repeat for this exercise for 10 minutes.

278 Level 7: Swing and Hit

Props A large, soft ball and a lightweight plastic bat for each pair

Divide the group into pairs or have the players choose partners.

Tell the children: Practice pitching and batting with a partner. Repeat this exercise for 15 minutes or until each child has hit the ball several times.

Tip With a larger group, children can take turns batting.

How to Teach Rhythm

any size

Except as noted

Having a sense of rhythm is something you can teach children, especially at this age. Rhythm doesn't just mean learning to dance. We can have rhythm in basketball, tennis, and gymnastics and even rhythm to our day.

Activities involving rhythm teach children about their bodies and improve their coordination. Preschoolers' sense of rhythm develops naturally as they learn rhymes and hand games.

Rhythm, Timing

Tell the children: We will begin by singing and clapping out a song like "Twinkle, Twinkle, Little Star." Then, without singing, clap out the song and listen to the beat of the clap. I will now clap the rhythm of a different well-known children's song. [Clap the rhythm of a song like "Row, Row, Row Your Boat."] Can you tell which song I am clapping?

Level I: Feel the Beat

Place a child on your lap; let older children stand on your feet. Be sure to hang on to the child's hands.

Tell the children: We are going to listen to music, and we will sway side to side with the beat of the music. As we listen, clap out the beat of the music. Do this until the end of the song.

Tip Play different types of music, varying the tempos and beats.

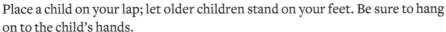

Level 2: Jump the Beat

Play music that preschoolers enjoy listening to like The Wiggles or Raffi.

   Tell the children: Jump up in the air when you hear a strong beat in the music. Repeat this for several songs.

 ## Level 3: Tap Out the Beat

Props   A table or other hard surface

Tell the children: Listen to the music, using the table as a drum find the beat and tap it with your hands on the table. Do this for 1 full song.

 ## Level 4: Stomp the Beat

Tell the children: Stomp your feet or clap your hands to music. March in place, stomp side to side, twirl, or rock back and forth to the beat. Do this for 1 full song.

 ## Level 5: Bounce to the Beat

Props   A large vinyl ball for each participant

Tell the children: Bounce a ball to music. Have the whole group or the entire family do this activity at the same time. Listen to the beat that is created by the bouncing balls. Do this for 1 full song.

Level 6: Musical Chairs

Props A chair and a name card for each participant

Set up the chairs in a circle with each child's name card on the seat of a chair. To keep the game interesting, move the cards to different chairs each time.

Tell the children: When the music starts, everyone begins moving around the chairs. When the music stops, find and sit in the chair with your name on it. Play this game for 3 minutes.

 Level 7: Musical Parade

Props A kitchen utensil or other piece of kitchen equipment for each participant

Gather pots, pans, wooden spoons, or any other kitchen utensil or piece of equipment that can double as a musical instrument. All players must have an instrument.

Tell the children: As I tap out a slow beat with my kitchen spoons, march to it and add to the beat with your instruments. As I pick up the tempo, you can simply walk to the beat. When I tap out an even faster tempo, run to the faster beat. Repeat this for up to 2 minutes.

Level 8: Freeze Dance

This game is fun when you get lots of people involved. Choose any style of music. If you want the children to move faster, choose music with a faster tempo.

Tell the children: When the music plays, begin to dance. When the music stops, you must freeze in position until the music starts again. Do this for 1 song.

288 Level 9: Interpretative Dance

Props Costumes

The world offers us many styles of dance. Introducing the children to a variety of styles will open up their imaginations to the world of dance. Select music that has a definite style to it, but allow your child's imagination to interpret the dance. Try using music from The Nutcracker Suite.

Tell the children: Dance to the music, using whatever steps you choose. Use your imagination to create new moves.

Tip You may want to record the performance on video.

289 Level 10: The Feather Dance

Props Feathers

Give each child one feather from a bag of colored feathers to "feather dance" with. Later, when the music is finished, throw the entire bag of feathers into the air. Let the players have fun gathering up their own little bunches of feathers.

Tell the children: While the music plays, keep your feather in the air by blowing on it.

290 Music Video

Props A stage; costumes; make-up; fake musical instruments

Choose music that preschoolers enjoy like music from The Wiggles. Someday you may be able to share these videos at their wedding receptions.

Tell the children: We are going to create our own music video. We will choose a song to lip sync and dance to and also use costumes, a stage, and make-up. Each of us can play a specific role in the video like a singer, dancer, or musician.

Some Classic Dances and Single Steps

Following are very watered-down versions of the original dances, but they will nonetheless help teach children a sense of timing and rhythm. The steps I have written down here are similar to the man's steps because, typically in ballroom dancing, the woman dances backward. If children want to learn ballroom dancing more seriously beyond this, many dance studios throughout the country offer that. Meanwhile, if the children find some of the single dance steps challenging as well, break them down in to slow patterns and keep practicing. They will need these coordination movements to advance into *303 Kid-Approved Exercises and Active Games*.

 ## 291 Knee Pops

This movement teaches children weight transfer from one foot to the other and coordination. Before starting the game, turn on some music.

Tell the children: Stand with your weight on both feet. As you listen to the music, "pop" your knee by bending it slightly forward. Immediately straighten your knee and do this movement with your other knee, continuing this alternating movement pattern until the end of this song. As your knee "pops," your hips will begin to shake too.

Variation Challenge the children by asking them to perform double knee pops on one knee and then repeat the movement with the other knee.

 ## 292 Circle Dance

Tell the children: Everyone join hands, and stretch out in the shape of a circle facing the center. While still holding hands, walk forward to the center, and now walk backward to where you started. Again, everyone walk forward to the center, and now walk backward to where you started. Still holding hands, everyone slide sideways to the right while facing the center. Now stop, and then everyone slide sideways to the left. Now drop hands and run forward to the center and sit down. Repeat this series of movements 2 times.

 ## Fox Trot

The fox trot begins almost the same way as the waltz, but has a slightly different count and moves to the left instead of the right. The kids do not need partners; just have them learn the footwork on their own.

Tell the children: Step forward with your left foot, and as you step forward count "1, 2." Now bring your right foot next to your left foot, counting "3, 4." Now your left foot steps to the left and your right foot follows quickly, counting "5, 6."

Tip Once your child learn the movements, you use these words to help him learn the rhythm: "Slow, slow, quick, quick."

 ## Heel-to-Bottom Jump

Tell the children: Begin with both feet together and your hands by your sides. Bend your knees, and squat down until you can place your hands on the floor just between and below your legs for balance. Then push off the floor and jump straight up into the air, bringing your heels toward your bottom and landing with your knees bent. Repeat this movement 3 times.

 ## Cat Walk

Prop A wall

Tell the children: Stand along one wall. Now walk across the room crossing one foot across and in front of the other before doing the same thing with your other foot. Be sure not to do this movement too quickly, so you don't trip over your own feet. Repeat this series of movements 2 times across the space.

Enchufla

Divide the group into pairs or have the players choose partners.

An enchufla is a basic salsa dance move that allows a participant to switch places with their partner.

Tell the children: Face your partner and hold both of her hands. Twirl around in a circle slowly. After doing this for 10 seconds, change directions and repeat again for 10 seconds.

Tip Don't let the children spin too quickly.

Chicken Dance

Music "The Chicken Dance Song"

Show the participants the steps as you describe them.

Tell the children: Stand in a circle, Open and close your hands and pretend they are your beaks. Now "chirp" your fingers 4 times (4 counts). Now make your arms look like wings by tucking your hands in your armpits and flap your wings 4 times. Now wiggle your "tail feathers" down to the floor 4 times and then clap your hands 4 times. Repeat all of the same movements along with the music 3 more times.

Gancho

Divide the group into pairs or have the players choose partners.

Tell the children: The word *gancho* means "hook" in Spanish. Hook your right arm into your partner's right arm. At the same time, both of you spin around. Try using the opposite arm, too.

Step Slide

Tell the children: Facing forward with your feet together and your knees bent, move to your right by pushing your right foot along floor to the right and then bringing your left foot over to the right until it is next to the right foot. You should also change directions, and when you move to your left, you lead with your left foot. Do this until the end of the song we are listening to.

Flick Kick

Demonstrate this movement with your wrist first so the children can understand how the movement should look when done with an ankle.

Tell the children: Kick forward from the knee with your right foot, flicking your ankle upward so the toes come up. Repeat this movement for 30 seconds, and then switch legs and repeat it for another 30 seconds.

Inside Turn

Divide the group into pairs or have the players choose partners.

Tell the children: Player 1, hold your partner's left hand in your right hand and have her turn toward you for an inside turn. Now switch roles and take turns being the turner. Repeat this exercise for 30 seconds.

 Outside Turn

Divide the group into pairs or have the players choose partners.

Tell the children: Player 1, hold your partner's left hand in your right hand and have him turn away from you for an outside turn. Now switch roles and take turns being the turner. Repeat this exercise for 30 seconds.

Rond

Tell the children: Rond is a ballet term. From a standing position, point your right toe out to the right side and draw a semicircle to the right on the floor. Repeat this 10 times and then do the same movement with your other leg.

Alphabetical
List of Games

List of Games Arranged by Specific Categories

Games Requiring a Large Space

4	Goin' Crazy	109	Core Challenge
31	Simon Says	111	Let's Dance
32	Graveyard Game	112	Leg Challenge
59	Slithering Lizard	113	Yoga-Class Combination
77	Walk and Jump	114	Strut, Tuck, and Roll
78	Forward and Backward	115	Tricky Legs
79	Toe-Tapping	116	A Sweaty Head
82	Hop and Roll	117	Animal Legs
83	Shuffling Jacks	118	Funny-Looking Combination
84	Pop and Slide	119	Lucky Lizards
85	Kick and Hop	120	Toe, Toe, Tootsies
86	Soar Like an Airplane	121	Skip, Straddle, Kick
87	Frog Legs	122	Go Backward
88	Dizzy Dance	123	Water Friends
90	Leap and Crawl	124	Cardio Moves
91	Flicker	125	What Am I?
92	Ballet Legs	126	Aerobic Challenge
93	Skip, Twirl, and Jump	144	Freeze Tag
94	Make Me Laugh	146	Level 1: One Step at a Time
95	Step, Swing, and Hold	147	Level 2: Side Step
96	Kickin' Tootsies	148	Level 3: Run with Me
97	Slide and Roll	149	Level 5: Adding On
98	Tuck and Jump	150	Level 5: A for Agile
100	On the Farm	151	Level 6: Run Like Grandma
101	Broadway Show	152	Level 7: No Arms
102	Getting-Fit Combination	153	Level 8: Interval Runs
103	Down Under	154	Level 9: Take a Hike
104	Swimming Combination	155	Level 10: Go to the Beach or the Pool
105	Worms		
106	Reptile Challenge	156	Relay Races
107	Coordination Challenge	158	I Wonder
108	Get Down	159	Red Light, Green Light

Games in Which Physical Contact Might Be Involved

Games Requiring an Exercise Mat

Games Requiring Props

Games Requiring Musical Accompaniment

Printed in the USA
CPSIA information can be obtained
at www.ICGtesting.com
JSHW082211140824
68134JS00014B/549